# ANALYZE PEOPLE WITH DARK PSYCHOLOGY

*Complete Beginner's Guide to Dark Psychology. It Includes Manipulation, Art of Persuasion, Mind Hacking, and Body Language*

© **Copyright 2022 - All rights reserved**.

This document is geared towards providing exact and reliable information in regard to the topic and issue covered.

- From a Declaration of Principles which was accepted and approved equally by a Committee of the American Bar Association and a Committee of Publishers and Associations.

In no way is it legal to reproduce, duplicate, or transmit any part of this document in either electronic means or in printed format. All rights reserved.

The information provided herein is stated to be truthful and consistent, in that any liability, in terms of inattention or otherwise, by any usage or abuse of any policies, processes, or directions contained within is the solitary and utter responsibility of the recipient reader. Under no circumstances will any legal responsibility or blame be held against the publisher for any reparation, damages, or monetary loss due to the information herein, either directly or indirectly.

Respective authors own all copyrights not held by the publisher.

The information herein is offered for informational purposes solely and is universal as so. The presentation of the information is without contract or any type of guarantee assurance.

The trademarks that are used are without any consent, and the publication of the trademark is without permission or backing by the trademark owner. All trademarks and brands within this book are for clarifying purposes only and are owned by the owners themselves, not affiliated with this document.

# Table of Contents

Introduction
Chapter 1: Manipulation Examples
Chapter 2: Basics of Manipulation
Chapter 3: NLP
Chapter 4: Persuasion Weapons and Secrets
Chapter 5: Manipulation
Chapter 6: How to Defend From Manipulation
Conclusion

## Book 2: DARK PSYCHOLOGY

Introduction
Chapter 1: How to Analyze People
Chapter 2: How to Read People
Chapter 3: The Eyes, Mirror of the Soul
Chapter 4: How Our Body Speaks
Chapter 5: How to Show Yourself to Others
Chapter 6: How to Identify Insecurity
Chapter 7: Benefits of Personality Analysis
Chapter 8: How Body Language Enhances Your Mind
Conclusion

# Introduction

The art of manipulation is not really about influencing people into doing what you want them to do. Instead, it is about getting them to want to do what you want them to do. The most important question here is, "How do you get people to want to do what you want them to do?"

Well, the first trick is to learn their true desires and then reverse engineer them towards the goal you wish to accomplish. One thing you must bear in mind is that the closer you are to a person, the easier it is for you to manipulate them. If you want to test your manipulation skills, the first person to do this with is your romantic partner.

Think of manipulation as persuasion.

The truth is, you must be willing to persuade people and make them feel like it was their choice all this while. Generally, men seek perfectionism while women see wholeness. You may be thinking, "What does this even mean?" the truth is that men are easily persuaded by mastery and an ego linked to improvement. When you display uncertainty on whether or not a man can improve, you are simply taunting his ego in such a gentle way that contributes to progress.

On the other hand, women seek balance in various areas of life—especially relationships with family and friends. Therefore, when you suffocate time you stir up a burning desire to bring balance. The truth is, we all need balance, sacrifice, and focus in life. According to statistics, women tend to lean more towards balance, while men lead more towards perfectionism.

Amid persuasion tactics, you must not disobey the law of cognitive bias—otherwise referred to as liking and loving tendency.

There are 2 major ways you can test delusion—doing things in the wrong order still means the wrong thing (also referred to as miss-prioritization.) or setting expectations of the outcome by putting in the wrong input. With people, you must learn their personality type, how they react to different surroundings and their boundaries.

Here's the point—the mental frameworks are out of the way. One way you are going to get them to do the thing is to lead with a reward. People love it when they feel like it's their choice and that triggers the release of dopamine—otherwise known as the reward. They want to know how the thing you are telling them to do is going to benefit them. The trick is not to tell them to do it directly. According to research, at least 90% of the time, people hate being told what to do. The best thing to do is to help them to the same conclusion following their path. The most rewarding thing is them knowing that it was their idea—when, in fact, it was yours. Therefore, you must let them own it. The toughest part is attaching that reward to the thing because if they don't understand how something is of benefit to them, there is a high likelihood that they will never do it.

Once you manage to successfully manipulate others you must not expose yourself because this goes against the liking and loving tendency, causing people to cut you off — and that is the last thing you want. You must maintain consciousness of how you make them feel and try to persuade for the best and not for evil.

## Techniques Used by Manipulators to Gain Control

Psychopaths are not villains we watch in movies or read in morality takes — they are real and walk amongst us at home and in offices appearing to us as normal colleagues. According to one study, at least 3-4% of business leaders are psychopaths. The same thing applies to narcissists. Science has shown some evidence that a little bit of narcissism goes a long way in aiding business success.

As you go about your business each day, there is a chance that you will meet a few truly toxic narcissists and psychopaths who will try to manipulate you in one way or the other. You must understand how such people can manipulate others. Here are a few techniques:

### Gaslighting

This is a manipulative technique that can be described in various ways. These include 3 key phrases:

- "That did not just happen".
- "You imagined it".
- "Are you insane?"

Well, gaslighting is one of the most common and insidious manipulative tactics because it aims at distorting and eroding people's sense of reality. In other words, it eats away your ability to trust yourself, inevitably disabling you from seeing the justification in calling out your abuser.

How then can you fight back?

The best thing is for you to ground yourself in your reality. One of the ways you can do this is to take time and write down exactly what happened, talk to a friend, or reiterate your experience to a support system that can help you counter the effects of gas lighters.

### Projection

Think about it — have you ever met someone so toxic that claims all the mess that surrounds them is your fault and not theirs?

Well, that tactic is referred to as projection.

Well, the truth is that we all have done this at someone's point in our lives. But the difference between us and narcissists or psychopaths is that they do it a lot. They simply use projection as a defense mechanism to displace the responsibility of their negative behaviors and qualities by ensuring that they attribute all of it to another person.

What is the solution then?

Well, it's simple—try as much as you can not to project your empathy or sense of compassion onto a toxic individual. Also, you mustn't own any of the toxic person's projections. When you project your conscience and value system onto others, this has a potential outcome of being met with more exploitation.

## Generalizations

Let us consider an instance where you tell a coworker that they sometimes fail to consider the long-term ramifications of their financial decisions. Then they go ahead and tell everyone that you called them "loose cannon." You realize that this might blow up on you if several conditions come into play. Your psychopath of a colleague goes to the boss and tells them that you said the deal is a "wreck."

What is going on?

Well, the truth is that your nemesis did not only understand you, but they also had no interest in understanding you.

One thing you must note is that malignant narcissists are not intellectual masterminds. Most of them are intellectually lazy. Instead of taking the time to consider another person's perspective, they simply choose to generalize everything you say by making a blanket statement that does not consider the nuances of your argument. They choose not to consider the different perspectives you paid homage to.

To counter this you must hold onto your truth and resist the urge to generalize things. Instead, they realize that they are, in fact, a form of black and white illogical thinking.

## Moving Goalposts

Even though you offer them all the evidence you need to validate your argument or meet their requests, they will set up another expectation and demand proof.

You must avoid playing such a game. You are the only one that needs to validate and approve yourself. You are enough, and the last thing you want is to let someone make you constantly feel small, deficient, and unworthy.

## Changing the Subject

When you are saying something, and someone keeps changing the topic, it sounds innocent enough. However, in the hands of a manipulator, changing the subject is one way to keep off responsibility. A narcissist will not want you to stay on the topic because the last thing they want is you holding them accountable for something. In that case, they will find ways to reroute the conversation to benefit them.

If you are not careful, this sort of thing can go on forever. It can make it impossible to engage in a relevant issue. The best way to counter this is to the user the "broken record technique" when fighting back. In other words, you must keep stating the facts without allowing yourself to yield to distractions.

Let is stay focused on the real issue here. If you lack interest in this, then you can choose to disengage and spend your time and energy on something a little more "constructive."


## Name-Calling

Each one of us has been called names at some point in our lives. We have been dealing with this long enough, but that does not make it any less destructive. Trust me, this thing might have started from the time you were in kindergarten, but it goes all the way to presidential politics!

Even if you have encountered bullies since childhood, you mustn't tolerate it. End any interaction that entails name-calling and tell your manipulator that you will not tolerate it. Don't even try to take it all in — as most people do. Realize that the reason they resort to name-calling is that they are deficient and are trying to distract you from what matters.


## Smear Campaigns

When a toxic person cannot control the way, you perceive yourself, they choose to control how others see you. In other words, they resort to playing the martyr while everyone around you starts to label you as the toxic one. This is a smear campaign that is only preemptive to ensuring that they tarnish your reputation and slander your name.

Realize that at times, true evil geniuses will choose to divide and conquer — by pitting 2 or more people against one another.

The last thing you want is to allow them to succeed. You must record all forms of harassment and ensure that you don't rise to the bait. Do not allow their evilness to provoke you into stooping to their level and behaving just like them.

# Chapter 1: Manipulation Examples

Manipulation is the crucial point in dark psychology that aims at changing the perception and behavior of the subject. The manipulator uses various tactics to improve the thinking of the subject towards a particular situation, thing, person, or matter. Manipulators use different tactics like persuasion, brainwashing, and blackmailing to influence others to obey them.

The layman needs to know about manipulations that every one of you would have faced in your life. The manipulator's intention could be to get benefits from the subject or to harm them. The drawback of manipulation is that the manipulator does not care about the feelings and needs of the individual. Manipulators don't care about the subjects whether they get harmed physically or emotionally. They control other's minds by blackmailing or threatening them or whatever is necessary to overpower others.

Many times, subjects recognize that they are being manipulated, but they do not consider it as the form of tactic used to control or harm them.

Some people consider manipulation as a way of leading a successful life. In this regard, manipulators use a set of manipulations and tricks to overpower the subject. Some of these techniques/manipulations are as follows:

## Lying

Manipulators are involved in false stories, exaggerations, or partial truths. They hide the real side of the story from the subject to make them comply with them. For example, brands usually provide false statements about their product services, which they do not offer in reality.

## Rotating the Truth

Manipulators spin the facts to match with their views. This is often done by the politicians who twist the truth to best fit their policies and rules. Manipulators in this type of tactic justify their statements by providing fake justifications and clarifications. They spin the statements to match their ideas or views even when they do not involve any original basis.

## Withdrawal of Affection

Manipulators often persuade people by withdrawing friendship and love from the subject. In this way, they mentally torture the subject and make them comply with them. This happens in a romantic relationship when any of the partners do not comply with others. When any of the partners no longer engages in affection, love, or compliance, the other may automatically adapt to the habits and behaviors that the manipulator wants them to exhibit.

## Sarcastic Jokes

The influencer uses sarcastic jokes over their subject in front of others to show them how powerful they are. Negative and mean comments are given to the subject in front of everyone to show the manipulator's power. Many individuals who want to avoid these negative and sarcastic comments in front of everyone often engage in the behavior that the manipulator wants them to exhibit.

## Make Subject Feel Helpless

Innocent people often are the victim of this type of tactic. Manipulators make the subject feel helpless for their lousy life. At the helplessness stage, when the influencer thinks that they are helpless and there is no one to share their problems or whatsoever. At that point, the influencer comes as the helper of the individual. Then influencer takes advantage of the helplessness of the subject and makes the victim obey them.

## Use of Aggression

To show dominance and power over individuals, the manipulator uses aggression as a tool to take control over others. The manipulator engages in aggression, the temper outburst to frighten the intended person. Thus, the individual becomes frightened and focuses more on controlling the manipulator's anger instead of talking about the original issue.

## Plays the Role of Victim

The manipulator at this level swaps the part and acts like a victim to gain others' sympathies. They go to the intended person and gain their sympathies in this way. The individual automatically gets inclined towards the needs and demands of the manipulator and fulfills their desires. This is the most widely used influencing technique by pretenders.

## Pretending Ignorance

In this type of tactic, the influencer does not want to let you know what they want. The manipulator will pretend that they are ignoring the individual. This is done to divert the attention of the individual toward the manipulator. The individual at some time will comply with the manipulator to make them pay attention.

## Threats

One of the most frequently used influencing tactics is abusing and punishing others. The influencer often involves aggressive behaviors and threats to the individual. Moreover, the influencer punishes the individual to overpower them and make them obey. Many times, the influencer involves physical violence, mental abuse, and many other punishing behaviors.

## Emotional Blackmailing

Emotional blackmailing is another manipulating technique that the influencer uses to overpower the individual. The manipulator might trap the individual by emotionally blackmailing them that they are selfish and don't care about what's going on in the influencer's life. The tactic helps the influencer trap the individual better and make them anxious and confused.

## Pretending Empathy

As you all know, influencers or manipulators don't usually empathize with people, but if they do so it is for their good. They pretend as if they love or empathize with the individual, but in fact, they do not. This helps pretenders incline individuals towards them. This is a great tactic to make someone obey you in a very sound and calm manner.

## Positive Reinforcement

As you know, gifts and presents are considered a sign of love and charm for everyone. Gifts enhance and change the thinking pattern of the individual toward the giver. Positive reinforcement is a technique used by many people; it involves giving gifts, favorite toys, money, and many other favorites of the person. For example, parents give their child their favorite sports car upon graduating with good grades; teachers give gifts to their students when they do homework or tasks efficiently.

## Minimization

This tactic is used to minimize the effect of manipulators' wrongdoings. Manipulators try to convince the individual that what they did wasn't as harmful or bad as it seemed to be. However, when an individual makes the manipulator confront their wrong deeds, the manipulator might consider it as the over-exaggeration or overreaction from the individual. In other words, minimization involves the reduction of the adverse effects of the manipulator's wrongful acts.

# Chapter 2: Basics of Manipulation

Mental manipulation is perhaps one of the most common forms of manipulation people will try to use on you. As a result of how often it occurs, it can be somewhat challenging to know when a behavior should be considered mental manipulation or not.
Simply put, think of mental manipulation as mind games, mind games that people will try and play with you. Some people will try to play these games at any chance they have no matter who you are and no matter the consequences they may face as a result of their behavior, especially in the workforce we all know someone who will try and kiss up to the boss or put you down to make themselves look more appealing.

## Manipulators Follow a Pattern

The good news is that most of these tactics all follow a similar pattern in how they work, and as a result, once a few are understood it becomes much easier to understand them all as a group. This will be the primary focus, what kind of forms mental manipulation can take on, how it hides and what to do when you encounter it.
With each form of manipulation mentioned building on the next and so on. That last step of knowing what to do when you encounter manipulation is perhaps the hardest because. The reason for its difficulty comes from the fact that an in-depth understanding is the most necessary component of defusing it, and that can be difficult to have. But once you gain this knowledge, you can even perhaps use it for yourself in certain situations to try and gain something difficult peacefully or to make money. Take the real estate industry, for example, most of what will drive someone to buy a house is not usually always if it has the latest and greatest build materials, but the things that "matter" to them these things that matter are based on simple primitive emotions and realtors know this.

# Flattery Will Get You Everywhere

Moving on from lying and deceit, I would like to talk about one of the more effective methods of manipulation, and that is flattery. Flattery is an idea we think of when the thought of relationships comes to mind. The husband and wife out to dinner are joyfully juking and jiving with each other. Or someone at a bar, trying to pick up a girl. On the surface, that is technically flattery as in its simplest terms, flattery just defines a behavior where someone goes out of their way to give platitudes to you regardless if they're truthful or not. Because of how flattery can make us feel good about ourselves, it can be challenging to view it as something manipulative or bad. And the strange truth is that flattery or outright being a kiss-up is not always a bad thing if you want to get ahead in something. As mentioned, prior, this is especially true if you are trying to win a girl.
To be honest, flattery, in its milder form, is one of the integral parts of our whole courting process as humans. Flattery used well in the workforce, for example, can be extremely advantageous for the person doing it. As it allows them to try and endear themselves to their boss or other co-workers. In doing this, they will gain those individual's trust allowing them more upward movement within the company.
The issue with flattery is that it can be used to create relationships on pretenses, i.e., it lures someone into a false sense of security about how someone views them. Trust like this that is easily generated is always something you should be cautious about. For example, you start dating a man, and he is overly flirtatious and goes seemingly too far to make you feel good then perhaps consider that maybe his intentions are not quite pure. The line between flattery and genuine true compliments lies first in you knowing yourself and your self-worth. If you are a strong, confident person then you will know if someone is trying to compliment you in a way that seems to both tries too hard and also be untrue.
So, remember, general flattery is not always a bad thing, but it can be a segue for someone into getting you to give them a false sense of trust, which is not always the best. Remembering this and what kind of behavior to look for will help you avoid being a victim of a manipulator in the future. As the line between simple flattery to be friendly and flattery for malice has a fine line, just as anything does.

# Remember—Manipulation Isn't Necessarily Bad

As I mentioned earlier, not all manipulation has to be used for bad purposes. Some forms of manipulation we encounter regularly, such as advertising and mass media can be used for good, so much so that they can make someone a profit. Or they can be used in the corporate world to climb up the ladder of hierarchy. In simple terms, at times, it can be required that you grease some palms and perhaps act a certain way to get ahead.

Using manipulation techniques such as bending the truth or flattery may be required here to give you an advantage over the competition. In this case, it could be argued that it can be morally permitted due to the honest fact that if you don't try to push your way into these positions, someone else will. At this point, you are only playing the game that everyone else is playing by going out of your way, being friendly to your boss, or bending the truth in how you present your accomplishments. Yes, you are using manipulation by giving your boss the impression that an assignment you just completed may be better than it really might be.

Is that form of manipulation so bad? All you are doing is simply leveling the playing field. This type of behavior is less manipulation and more in line with the idea of being persuasive or charismatic.

The difference here is you are using charm and ingratiation to convince someone further toward your line of thinking regardless of what that may be. It is still their decision in the end. All your doing is guiding and influencing them. This is far different from coercion, where you are using subtle threats and fear to get what you want. An example of this type of coercion would be lying to your boss about the performance of another coworker to put them down and allow you to get a position that they currently hold.

# Chapter 3: NLP

## What Is NLP?

When you hear of the term NLP. What's the first thing that comes to mind? Probably something straight out of Star Wars, right? Well, you might be dead wrong. This is an acronym for Neuron-Linguistic Programming. This is one of the prevalent themes that exist in the quest for persuasion and dark psychology. Over the years, NLP has often had different meanings, it could be defined as a particular attitude for a sense of adventure and curiosity to know more about the types of communication that can influence others as well as ourselves offering us a rare chance to better ourselves or juts grow as individuals. It has also been defined as a methodology purely based on the notion that all the behaviors we have as human beings have a certain structure and process. These processes, as well as structures, may be replicated, taught, learned as well as changed. It has also been defined as being a theme that has slowly evolved into an innovative technology, which allows us to organize our thoughts and ideas in certain ways to achieve a particular set of results that would normally be out of our reach. Perhaps the best and easily understood definition of NLP would be that it is a sort of learning system that develops a particular language through making connections between various senses of your body. It has been in existence for more than 40 years and has proved to be efficient.

Neuron-Linguistic Programing is not usually based on the notion of new-age mantras or hanging some herbal trees in your room to be more notches with your inner self. This theme of dark psychology is usually based on some solid psychological principle. It is a rapid form of psychological therapy which is capable of addressing the myriad of problems that we are doomed to face in our daily lives such as depression, some form of phobias, or any form of negative habits we may have.

NLP has some other distinct features that we shall briefly mention. NLP is not usually based on any statistics. The reason for this is that statistics may not be able to predict a person's subjective experience. This is because human being's subjective experiences are not understood by the external sensory experience. Another distinct feature of NLP is that it is not linear. This enigmatic theme sent usually limits itself to any particular linear cause-effect thinking. This happens to be so because it has a preference for whole system thinking. This system tends to be self-organizing and too complex for useful linear cause-effect analysis.

NLP can also be said to be efficient as is now familiar to you; NLP usually does not pursue case effects of an unresolvable nature. Such question-answer sequences like… Why? NLP prefers to ask a useful set of questions such as how? What? When? Who? Since this has few expectations, it is of the view that taking the long personal history of the individual for some casual analysis is a colossal waste of time. It will, however, opt to take that route when it is appropriate to direct as it's presently coded in a person's mind. This dark theme has a set of powerful tools that, when utilized correctly by the individual who has come across them, can make some drastic positive change to their on-going experience of personal history as well as its meaning, patterns which emerged as a result of one's own life experiences and other factors connected with their past. This is however devoid of the use of any drugs, hypnosis, or years of analysis.

## How to Use NLP in Relationships and Manipulative People?

Now that we know all that NLP entails, let us see how it can be used in relationships. The first way this theme can help you better your relationships is by enabling you to be a good listener. NLP enables you to show a more sincere interest in whatever may be happening in the other person's life. Another way NLP betters relationships is by making you put yourself in another person's shoes. Being in the world of the other person requires you to listen openly. In other words, you're listening and you're just listening. This can take some practice since most individuals tend to listen partly while preparing or rehearsing what they say next internally. NLP also allows you to not focus on the bad side of a person but instead so the good. There are many of them and you have a decision to pay more attention to their fine points or imperfections. The more you find the fine points of a person and concentrate on them, the greater your regard for them.
NLP also allows one to be more empathetic rather than sympathetic. Empathy means understanding and feeling their difficulties without trying to engage unless requested. Sympathy, being sorry for them, is disrespectful and shows that you feel that they have no resources alone to deal with their problems. Relationships are fostered by NLP since they push someone to keep in touch with their loved ones. Even if you were together several hours before, maybe at breakfast, how about a one-minute telephone call, asking how your day is going and telling you to think about them? Or a one-line email or text email? Keep in touch with those at a distance, too. If nourished, long-distance relationships may last for decades. The connection will be maintained and maintained by the occasional letter, card, telephone call, or email. NLP makes it easier for one to accept the flaws of others. Identify and tolerate the weaknesses and imperfections of a person. After all, "weaknesses" are subjective assessments based on your view of the world. And remember that there are no perfect people — most of us work from time to time to reduce the number and magnitude of our imperfections — this is a lifelong project.

# Chapter 4: Persuasion Weapons and Secrets

The basis of persuasion is to direct the other person to the thought you desire and to make it normal in their basic belief and vision system. To simplify, it is to make the other person think the way you want. That's exactly what it means to convince. If the other person thinks the way you want, you can take the action that you want to take, that is, buying a product or consuming a product.
Located below are techniques to persuade and convince effectively. Persuasion techniques are not limited to these but they are important for efficiency.

## Creating Needs

One of the best methods of persuasion is to create a need or to reassure an old need. This question of need is related to self-protection and compatibility with basic emotions such as love. This technique is one of the biggest trumps of marketers in particular. They try to sell their products or services using this technique. The kind of approach that expresses the purchase of a product to make one feel safe or loving is part of the need-building technique.

## Touching Social Needs

The basis of the technique of touching social needs are factors such as being popular, having prestige, or having the same status as others. The advertisements on television are the ideal examples. People who buy the products in these advertisements think they will be like the person in the advertisement or they will be as prestigious. The main reason why persuasion techniques such as touching social needs are effective is related to television advertising is that many people watch television for at least 1–2 hours a day, and will encounter these advertisements.

# Meaningful and Positive Words

Sometimes it is necessary to use magic words to be convincing. These magic words are meaningful and positive. Advertisers know these positive and meaningful words intimately. They need to be able to use them. The words "New," "Renewed," "All Natural," "Most Effective" are the most appropriate examples of these magic words. Using these words, advertisers try to promote their products and thus make the advertisements more convincing for the liking of the products.

# The Foot Technique

This technique is frequently used in the context of persuasion techniques. The processing way is quite simple. You make a person do something very small first because you think they can't refuse it. Once the other person has done so, you will try to get them to do more, provided they are consistent within themself.
First, you sell a product to a person at a very low price, then, you get them to buy a product at higher prices. In the first step, you attract them to yourself, so you convince them to buy it. In the second step, you convince to buy products at a higher price. Their acceptance of a small thing will help you to fulfill the next big demand from you.
After accepting the small request from the other party, you feel a duty to make a big request from the same person. This is usually the case in human relations. For example, you agree when your neighbor comes and asks you if you can keep an eye on the shop for a few hours. If your neighbor comes to ask you to look at the shop all day, you will feel responsible and probably accept it. This means that the technique of putting a foot on the door is successfully applied.

# Orientation From Big to Small

The tendency to ask from big to small is the exact opposite of the technique of putting a foot on the door. The salesperson makes an unrealistic request from the other person. Naturally, this demand doesn't correspond to the real issue. However, the salesperson then makes a request that is smaller than the same person. People feel responsible for such approaches and they will accept the offer. Since the request is small, by accepting it, people have the idea that they will help the salespeople and the technique of moving from big to small requests works.

# Reciprocity

Reciprocity is a term for the mutual progress of a business. When a person does you a kindness, you feel the need to do them a favor. This is one example of reciprocity. For example, if someone bought you a gift on your birthday, you would try to pay back that gesture. This is more of a psychological approach because people don't forget the person who does something for them and they try to respond accordingly.

For marketers, the situation is slightly different from human relations. Reciprocity takes place here in the form of a marketer offering you an interim "extra-discount" or "extra" promotion… you are very close to buying the product introduced by the marketer because you think they offer a special offer.

# Making Limits for Negotiations

Setting a limit for negotiations is to provide an approach that will affect future rights. This is particularly effective when negotiating prices. For example, if you are trying to negotiate a price to sell a service, it might make more sense to start by opening the price from a higher number. Opening from a low number is not the right method because you have weakened your stretching share.

Even if the limitation for negotiations is not always useful, it's particularly useful in terms of price negotiation. Say the first number and get on with the bargaining advantage.

# Limitation Technique

The restriction technique is one of the most powerful methods to influence human psychology. You can see this mostly in places selling products. For example, if a store has a discount on a particular product, it may limit it to 500 products. This limitation can be a true limitation or a part of the limitation technique. So, you think that you will not find the product at that price again and you agree to buy that product at the specified price. The restriction technique is particularly useful in new products. As soon as a new product goes on sale, you can convince people to buy it for a limited time or by selling a limited quantity of products with extra promotions or discounts. People who think that the product will not be sold again at a similar price may choose to buy the product you have chosen thanks to the success of your persuasion technique.

Persuasion techniques are not limited to these. Different techniques can provide more successful results in various fields. However, most of the techniques we may encounter in our daily lives consist of the methods shown here. If you want to be a marketer, if you are trying to sell a product or service, you need to have detailed information about these techniques if you want to make them available.

## Difference Between Persuasion and Manipulation

There are many similarities between persuasion and manipulation as the 2 words confuse non-English individuals and natives too. There are many comparisons between the 2 concepts and because of the overlap, people think these 2 can be used interchangeably. There are convincing good people, and there are good manipulators. Both try to make sense and encourage others to accept their views. However, although there are similarities in manipulation to being able to persuade someone, there are differences that must be emphasized.

Particularly, persuasion is when an individual is led by someone else in a specific direction. You've managed to convince when you try to explain a certain way of behavior logically and correctly, and others accept your opinion that they think is of mutual benefit. If you have good marks on your test and you asked your mother for an expensive gift, you are trying to convince her to buy you a gift. This persuasion is convincing because it sees the logic behind your request and she buys the gift.

# Chapter 5: Manipulation

If you could force people to obey you, would you do it? If you could force the hand of someone else, even though you knew that they did not want to do what you were asking, would you be willing to do so? Perhaps you need to borrow $5,000 for a down payment on a car, but your parents are unwilling to give it to you. Maybe you want to borrow your friend's new motorcycle to experiment on it but they are reluctant because you do not have a license. How likely are you to make it a point to move forward? What if your friend is in a relationship with someone abusive or just not right for her? Would you do anything in your power to convince her to end the relationship?

All of that and more is possible with the power of manipulation. When you can manipulate people, you are effectively managing to influence the mind of the other person. You can figure out how best to control the other person and ensure that you can take over once and for all. You can use your understanding of the other person's mind to get them to do just about anything. If you can play your cards right, you can covertly access the mind of someone else, install all of the right strings and play the other person like a puppet.

This skill can be incredibly useful to you if you know what you are doing. You can figure out how best to take control of the mind of someone else. You can convince them to do your bidding, whether for your own or their benefit. This will introduce you to manipulation as a concept. You will learn how manipulation works as a concept. Lastly, you will be provided with several examples of types of manipulation that you may encounter in your daily life.

## Manipulation

By definition, manipulation is a form of social influence that is designed to change either behaviors or perceptions of other people through methods that are deceptive in some way. Usually, the purpose is to allow the manipulator to get what they want, even if it is at the expense of their target. Effectively, it is finding a way to coercively and secretly exploit someone else into doing what you want or need them to do.

When you manipulate someone else, you have an ulterior motive that you are pushing. You want to ensure that your desired result happens regardless of whether it impacts you versus your target. For example, telling your child that they must tell the truth or you are going to die would be a form of emotional manipulation. You are putting excessive weight on the consequence that would never happen to coerce your child into telling you something. You may be trying to get them to tell the truth but you are also doing so in a way that is emotionally harmful to the child.

Sometimes, manipulation is a bit more difficult to spot—it can be finding ways to use insecurities against the victim without them being spotted. No matter what, however, what holds true is that manipulation is designed to override everyone's inherent right to free will. This is not something to be proud of or to accept—if you are on the receiving end of manipulation, you should be trying to protect that free will as much as you can. If you are the manipulator, you may need to reconsider your motives and tactics. Controlling people is typically considered quite underhanded and cruel, and it should not be occurring on the regular, or at all if it can be avoided. It can be valuable to understand the art of manipulation to comprehend how the mind works or how manipulators will attack, but ultimately, the use of true manipulation is not recommended.

## The Process of Manipulation

People tend to believe that manipulation is effective for different reasons. They have different ideas about what makes manipulation effective. In particular, there are three criteria involving the manipulator that must be met to ensure that manipulation is successful. Ultimately, it is the manipulator that is primarily responsible for the manipulation and determining whether it will work, though certain personality traits tend to be particularly vulnerable to the attempts to manipulate. The 3 criteria that must be met to ensure successful manipulation are listed below.
Keep in mind that these 3 criteria being present are not a guarantee that the manipulation will always work. However, they must be present if it will work.

### Hiding True Intentions

If someone came up to you and said, "I am going to force you to buy me dinner," you would be likely to outright refuse. People tend to be contrarian—they will lean toward doing the exact opposite of what someone else is asserting that they do simply because they want to have their free will. Because of this, manipulation only really works well when the true intentions are hidden. This way, the victim is unaware of the manipulation taking place and is more likely to fall for it. They will be unsuspecting and, therefore, more susceptible as opposed to if they were already on guard and looking for any attempts to force their hands.

## Understanding Vulnerabilities

Ultimately, the only way that you can get to someone is if you know where their weak spots are. By taking advantage of the other party's weak spots, you can effectively figure out exactly how to present what you want to ensure they give it to you. For example, if you know that you are dealing with a people pleaser, you may make it a point to mention that you have this really important need that you want to figure out how to meet and word it in just the right way that cues the other person to ask if they can help. This is an example of a vulnerability. Others can include:

- They need to be given external approval.
- Fear of negative emotions.
- Unassertiveness.
- Struggling to know one's true self.
- Struggling with self-reliance.
- Feeling out of control.
- Being naïve.
- Lacking self-confidence.
- Being too conscientious.

Of course, there are other vulnerabilities as well, and you can begin to pinpoint more personal ones as well if you know what you are doing. Your job when manipulating others will be to figure out those vulnerabilities and use them.

## Ruthlessness

Ultimately, manipulation is quite often harmful to at least the party that is being victimized. In most cases, the one being manipulated stands to lose something, and most people feel guilty at the idea of costing someone else something personal. For this reason, the successful manipulator must not care about the other person enough to be able to shirk off the guilt that would come along with hurting them. For many people, they are simply too empathetic to completely disregard everyone else. For others, however, it becomes effortless to simply disregard any guilt over feeling like they have used the other party. They move on with their lives after getting what they want without ever batting an eye.

# Manipulation Tactics

Typically, manipulators exert some sort of control over their targets. They would have to truly get their way. However, no two manipulators are the same. Some may favor positive reinforcement, while others prefer to punish. No matter the method, there is no denying that the manipulation can be exhausting, unhealthy, and sometimes completely dangerous.

We will identify the five distinct tactics that manipulators tend to use. The tactics are sort of categories of different forms of manipulation—they are the most simplified form of classifying the techniques that you will be introduced to, and they use some sort of psychological tendency or process to control the other person.

## Positive Reinforcement

Rather than looking at positive as something good, think of positive as being provided or given something. When you are given positive reinforcement to encourage you to do something, you are introduced to some sort of motivator. You will get something as a direct result of your choice in action or to get you to do something.

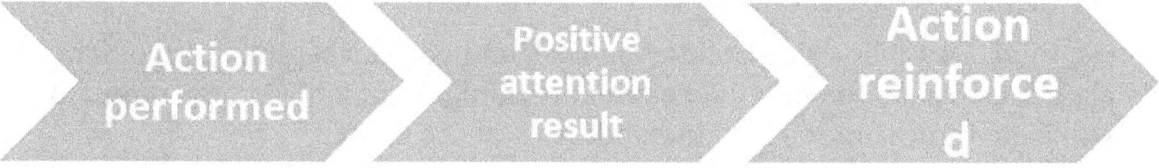

For example, one form of positive reinforcement is being given praise or a reward for completing a task as you were expected to do. In particular, during manipulation, you may be offered praise if you do the right thing without being asked or encouraged to do it. Ultimately, it is designed to encourage. Other forms of positive reinforcement include:

- Praise
- Public recognition
- Facial expressions
- Approval
- Love or affection
- Gifts

## Negative Reinforcement

Negative reinforcement, on the other hand, involves using negative situations with the removal from that negative situation as the reward. When you are provided negative reinforcement, you are effectively being told that if you do something, a negative situation will be remedied in some way. This uses the negative situation and the desire to be rescued from that negativity as the motivation to push you toward a certain action.

For example, imagine that you are in a bit of a bind—you may realize that you are $1,000 short for your bills in three days and be panicking. A manipulator may say that they will give you that $1,000 and therefore save you from the uncomfortable and terrifying potential of losing one's home. Another example could involve telling a child that they will not have to do the dishes if they do whatever you want instead.

## Intermittent Reinforcement

Intermittent reinforcement refers to only sometimes providing positive reinforcement. Doing so causes doubt, fear, and a desire to keep trying to fish for that approval or positive reinforcement that is desired. The absence of whatever is being offered up intermittently can cause people to work harder to get it.

Perhaps the easiest way to understand intermittent reinforcement is to look at gambling. In gambling, you are occasionally able to win, but most of the time, you lose. The occasional win and the knowledge that you have the chance to win are both enough for people to continually pour money into gambling, even though they are probably losing out on more money than they have ever won back.

This form of reinforcement may be the most effective—it causes the individual to effectively become addicted to the chase toward success or fulfillment. Think about an abusive relationship for a moment—the victim will oftentimes become addicted to the intermittent reinforcement of the honeymoon period within the cycle of abuse, and that is enough to keep the individual stuck.

# Chapter 6: How to Defend From Manipulation

There will always be people trying to shake your trust-people trying to instill self-doubt inside you. Such people would do their utmost to trick you into thinking that their beliefs are objective.

Manipulative people are not preoccupied with your needs. They worry about their interests. Once you allow manipulative people in your life, it can be tough to get rid of them. The trick is to have enough self-control to send the boot to dishonest people as soon as you see them. Here are a few ways to get rid of manipulative people from your life:

## Don't Fall Into Their Trap

Most of us come across instances where others seek to manipulate our thoughts, attitudes, or actions and take advantage of them to their benefit. In one such case, you fail to understand the real motive. The person mentally dominates you and you step into the pit. This emotional abuse often costs you a lot when you make some critical decisions under another person's control, and when it is too late you know it later.

You have to be conscious when a relationship sounds too good to be true. They are showering you with compassion, gratitude, admiration, congratulations, and affection. You feel like you live in a dream where everything seems perfect. They don't give you a reason to worry. You cannot find any flaws in them. Also, if anything goes wrong, they can begin to weep or feel sorry. You can have become the object of extreme intimacy and feel a passion for the fairy tale.

Individuals often succeed in manipulating their victims after intermittent reinforcement. We can avoid behaving in the same way while fighting back or demanding an answer. The explanation is that they are taking complete care of you now, so they say goodbye to the intermittent strengthening. We no longer need it. Manipulators have different faces and they can use many ways to get things done. The person may make an undertaking and later deny that you begin to doubt your perception. They do make you feel bad when you try hard to make them aware of their promise. They can employ shallow sympathy and burst into crocodile tears. Eventually, you end up trusting them and even doubting whether you listened correctly.

## Steer Straight Wherever Possible

A manipulator's actions typically vary according to the situation they're in. For instance, a manipulator may speak rudely to one person and act respectfully towards another the next moment. When you see these extremes frequently in a person it would be advisable to stay away from them, and you have to communicate with this that you will prevent from becoming a victim.

One way to identify a manipulator is to see if a person behaves differently and before other people with different faces. Although we all have a degree of this sort of social distinction, some psychological manipulators seem to dwell in extremes habitually, being highly polite to one person and gross to another, or helpless at one moment and fiercely violent at another. If you frequently experience this form of behavior from an adult, keep a healthy distance away, and avoid interacting with the person unless you have to. As described earlier, there are nuanced and deep-seated causes for persistent psychological abuse. Saving these is not your job.

There are some circumstances in which you can't entirely leave a relationship — most, usually whether that person is a parent or an extended family member. You probably cannot go cold turkey unless the individual causes serious harm or psychological damage. You need to accept this person completely for who they are and change your relationship standards accordingly. If they were someone you needed validation from before you would have to quit looking for their validation. Recognize that their advice is not something you need in your life if they were someone you received advice from. When they keep offering it you can thank them for it and then politely dump it. When setting these limits be as discreet as you can and do not tell the other person you are setting them. Creating this shift at your end will take some time, and when you get upset with the other person in the process you will have to deal with their reaction to that.

## Call Them Out on Their Actions

Manipulators are always difficult to deal with, but the worst is discreet manipulators. They will stay cool as a cucumber when confronted, and yet rigid and unbending. You may start to get frustrated when you start seeing their faulty reasoning. When you keep fighting with them you'll find it hard not to raise your voice a bit. You're going to start looking like the irrational one, and they're going to try to take back control in remaining calm based on their "maturity."

Defending yourself is tempting and trying to get the other person to see what is going on. But a true manipulator will not change their tune, and the more you give in to that urge to protect yourself the more they will twist your words more. Suppose you are in a situation with a true manipulator. In that case, the 2 goals for any conflict that is taking place should be to resolve and leave, whether leaving the current conversation or exiting the relationship. Evite threats, accusations, lose patience, accuse the other person of coercion, or become excessively emotional. Stick to honest, factual, and respectful declarations when you speak.

Some things require a high degree of intelligence, flexibility, or self-discipline when dealing with a manipulative person. You might not have the self-control to react without losing your temper and making things worse. If that's the case, accept this about yourself and take extra steps to avoid a tense confrontation (invite a mediator into the conversation, for example, or send an email instead of meeting in person so you have time to think through what you say).

## Touch Their Centre of Gravity

Manipulative people actively take advantage of their tactics against you. Through your enemies, they will become enemies and turn them against you. They're going to dangle some small reward in front of you and make you chase it relentlessly — they're going to take it away any time you get close to it. You will forever keep past acts above your head, and on, and on. Avoid letting those who exploit you use their tactics against you. Switch the tables in, instead. Build your plan and hit them where it hurts. When you are forced to deal with a dishonest person who, no matter how hard you try to avoid them, tries to make your life miserable, you have only one choice, find their center of gravity and destroy it. This center may be associates, followers, or subordinates to the deceptive individual. It may be a high-level talent or advanced knowledge of a particular area. They can manage it as a particular resource.

Figure out what their center of gravity is and make it yours anyway. Creating alliances with those close to them, hiring people to replace them with their skillsets and knowledge base, or siphoning away their precious assets. This will throw them off balance and push them to concentrate on managing their life, not yours.

## Believe in Your Decision

Many people are going around asking for the views of other people on anything. How do I want to do with my life? What am I fantastic at? Where am I, then? Avoid searching for other people so you can describe yourself. Define yourself. Believe in yourself. What distinguishes winners from losers is not the ability to listen to other people's opinions; it's the ability to listen to one's own opinions. You prevent dishonest people from influencing your life by setting up your values and keeping them tightly onto them. This will serve as a firewall to your convictions, keeping manipulators ostracized and out of your way.

## Try Not to Fit Right In

Keep reinventing yourself. One myth is the belief that continuity is somehow admirable or related to achievement. Manipulative people want you to be consistent so that they can count on you to advance their agendas. They want you to show up at 9 am every day and work at minimum wage for them.
Consistent assembly lines. The prison is uniform. Consistency is how they trap you in a shell. It's their way of manipulating you. The only way to stop being exploited is by consciously going against all the barriers other people seek to create for you. Hold on, trying to blend in. Instead, they're looking to stand out. Act to be different in some way, and never remain the same for too long. By design, personal growth needs a lack of consistency. Constant change is expected constant reinvention.

## Never Ask for Permission

We have been trained to ask for permission constantly. As a boy, we had to ask for everything we wanted — to be fed, changed, and burped. We had to get permission to go to the bathroom during the day, and we had to wait to eat lunch at a designated time and wait for our turn to play with toys. As a result, most people never cease to expect permission.
Employees around the world are waiting for a promotion and waiting for their turn to talk. Most are so used to being chosen that they sit in meetings in silence, afraid to talk out of turn or even lift their hands. It's a different way of living.

## Build a Greater Sense of Mission

Destiny-driven people aren't easily fooled. The reason manipulators in this world tend to prosper is that so many people lead a purposeless life. They're going to do anything. Because, somehow, nothing matters. People who lack intent waste time. There is no rhyme or explanation behind how they live their lives. We don't know where to go or why they are here. So, to avoid going insane, they're working in meaningless jobs and stuffing their minds full of celebrity gossip, reality television, and other useless types of media. They remain busy to avoid the desperate feeling of emptiness growing inside them. This profession and loneliness empower deceptive individuals.

# Chapter 7: The Dark Triad

Both psychologists and the regular public have been fascinated by the dark side of every human being for ages. Here, we are going to talk about the dark personality triad, which is nothing but a triangle formed by 3 personality traits that are independent but are very closely related to each other. And the only thing that is common among these 3 traits is that there is a certain level of evil connotation to all of them. These personality traits, when present in a person, make it challenging to have a conversation with them or deal with them, in general. Things become disagreeable very quickly, and these people are usually very arrogant, volatile, and domineering.

Now, coming to the triad, the 3 constituents are as follows — psychopathy, narcissism, and Machiavellianism. The people who have these qualities often have a toxic personality, and having intimate relationships with them is not only complicated but also derogatory to the other partner. The personality profiles of these people are created when the 3 qualities of the dark personality triad overlap.

Here is an example that might help you understand better:

A woman was once the subject of identity fraud. All her financial instruments like the credit card and her bank accounts were compromised in the process. She lived in an apartment where she had to pay monthly rent, and she lived with her boyfriend. Naturally, she was under a lot of stress as she was questioned regularly by the FBI, and this caused a tremendous amount of anxiety too. But even after all of this, the culprit couldn't be caught. But she thought that at least her fiancé was with her in all of this. He was very supportive of her. The fiancé also took the responsibility of paying monthly rent but from the money that the woman gave him. To cheer her up, he brought gifts from time to time. After a few days, the landlord of the apartment called the woman. He informed the woman about all the rents that she didn't pay. It was at that moment that she realized that the actual culprit in all of this was her fiancé. He was taking the money for the rent but was spending it on gifts. She was in complete denial because this was a case of extreme gaslighting. She couldn't believe the fact that it was her lover who was doing this to her.

## What Does the Dark Triad Mean?

So, let us have a more in-depth look into the dark triad and what it means. It was in the year 2002 when this term came into existence, and it was coined by Williams and Paulhus. You already know about the three characteristics that constitute this triad; we are going to go into the details.

It is said that anyone who has the traits belonging to the Dark Triad is showing subclinical symptoms. If we are to simplify this, it means that the person is not fully suffering from ASPD — Anti-Social Personality Disorder or NPD — Narcissistic Personality Disorder, but they are showing some symptoms.

You probably all have an idea of what narcissism means but here is a simplified description of it — it is a state where the person has a feeling of grandiosity, superiority, or entitlement. The person simply thinks that they are superior to everyone around them and they try to dominate everyone they meet. They are forever in the pursuit of ego gratification.

The major characteristic of Machiavellianism is the manipulatory attitude. People who have this trait are always focused on their gain in any circumstance whatsoever, and they always focus on their self-interest. They are also very duplicitous and calculating.

Lastly, if we are to explain psychopathy in simpler terms, then I would say that it is marked by a bold behavior where the person is anti-social, repulsive, and shows a lot of callousness.

## What Are the Characteristic Traits of People Belonging to the Dark Triad?

I have already explained the three traits of the dark triad separately but it is time that you understand the overall traits of a person who belongs to the dark triad.

- **Deception:** The first characteristic that can be easily spotted in these people is their deceptive nature. They do not have any amount of humility or honesty. They are greedy and are not sincere at all. When research was conducted on the 3 personalities individually it was found that all the personalities tend to cheat on their partners or family members when they think they are not going to get caught. On the contrary, when the risk factors were considerably high, it was found that Machiavellians and psychopaths continue to cheat. They are in the habit of continuous lying. On the other hand, if we are talking about narcissists, then instead of being dishonest intentionally, they are more prone to self-deception.
- **Callousness:** As you must have understood by now, people who belong to the Dark Triad, lack empathy. But to understand this concept better, research was conducted focusing specifically on affective empathy. Affective empathy simply means the power to respond to the emotions of others appropriately. The research concluded that the Dark Triad personalities lacked affective empathy as well. The results were quite creepy because these personalities felt good when they looked at currently sad people. Similarly, they automatically became negative whenever they saw someone who is positive or happy in their life. If we are to explain a bit more in detail, then psychopaths were found to be happy whenever they saw

someone was in fear. Similarly, both psychopaths and narcissists were found to be happy when they saw the expression of anger on people's faces.
- **Big 5 personality test:** This test was mainly done surrounding the qualities of openness, conscientiousness, agreeableness, neuroticism, and extraversion (Lewis R. Goldberg, 1992). Now, I just want to clarify something here because most people tend to get it wrong. Charisma and agreeableness are not the same things. Agreeableness is more like compliance, straightforwardness, and trustworthiness. All of these qualities are of the utmost importance when you want to form strong relationships. Conscientiousness was something that was found to be lacking in both psychopaths and Machiavellians. The level of neuroticism was the least in the case of psychopaths, and so basically, that is how you conclude them to be the most sinister of all. When it came to extraversion, narcissists were the ones who excelled in this criterion, and that is quite predictable too.

## Tips to Deal With People Who Have These Dark Triad Traits

If you think that someone in your life has the traits belonging to the Dark Triad, it can be hectic dealing with them, and so, here are some tips for you. You have to understand that the process is not easy, but it is possible with patience and the willingness to address these negative behaviors.

- **Handle the anger:** The first step will be to manage their aggression because it is something that is very often seen in people belonging to the dark triad. If those situations are not controlled, they can easily defuse into something bigger. It is quite easy to spot when someone is angry, even if it means that they are showing signs of passive-aggressive behavior (ignoring you or sulking). You can talk to them or distance yourself from them for a while, or you can figure out where all of that rage is coming from.
- **Don't let them bully you:** This is extremely important. It is not right or healthy if you have to withstand verbal or physical abuse. If you are in such a situation, you have to take a stand against it and take some action. Even if the abuse is indirect, for example, if the person is belittling you daily or criticizing you unnecessarily, you have to find a way to hold them accountable for their behavior.
- **Identify the manipulators:** We will go into greater detail about identifying manipulators in the next part of the book. But for now, you should know that when someone's Machiavellianism traits take the upper hand, they become manipulators. They will always be finding some excuse or the other for their hurtful behavior and try to make you say yes for things that you don't want to do.
- **Learn new skills:** Dealing with people with dark triad traits is no cakewalk, and so, you need special skills. It includes Emotional Intelligence, and you are going to learn about it in the latter part of this book. Once you acquire these skills, managing

these people would become easier, and you can also spot any kind of unwanted behavior at once.

# Chapter 8: Deception

The deception can include several different things, such as masking, camouflage, diversion, hand sleight, lies, and hiding. The agent will monitor the mind of the subject because the subject has faith in them. The subject believes what the agent says and could base their plans for the future and shape its universe on the stuff the agent told them. Deception is an omission and lying form of communication to persuade the subject's world to serve the agent the best.

## Types of Deception

The Interpersonal Deception theory outlined 5 different types of deception:
1. **Lies:** This is when the agent provides information that is different from reality. This knowledge is to be presented to the subject and the subject must understand it as the truth. The subject cannot understand that false information is being fed; if the subject understands that the data is wrong, they will not speak to the agent and they not be fooled.
2. **Concealment:** Is another form of deception that is very common. It happens when the agent intentionally or by conduct hides or omits information that is relevant to the subject for a particular context. The agent will not have lied to the client directly, but they will ensure that the important information needed is never a subject.
3. **Equivocation:** The agent makes conflicting, vague, and/or conditional statements. This is to make the subject confused and not understand what is happening. It can also save your face as an agent if the subject returns later, claiming they have been deceived.
4. **Exaggeration:** It happens when the agent overestimates a fact or stretches the facts to some degree to transform the story as it wishes. The agent may not lie to the subject directly, but they will make the current situation a bigger deal so that the subject bends to their will.
5. **Avoidance:** This occurs when manipulators don't give straight answers or move the conversation into a different topic utilizing diversion tactics. In a dialog, avoidance occurs by rambling, or otherwise talking endlessly in a meandering

fashion. So, their ultimate game is to confuse the target, which makes them question the true version. When a manipulator changes the topic, it can be gradual and not entirely obvious.

## Main Components of Deception

While deciding what factors display during deception may be difficult, certain components are typical of deception. It is often not obvious that these elements existed unless the agent told a blatant lie or was caught in deception. These are components that will be later remembered if the agent uses the deception technique in the right way:

1. **Camouflage**: This is the first dimension of deception. This is when the agent tries to conceal the facts so that the target does not know that the information is missing. This technique is often used when the agent uses half-truths when they are giving information about something. The subject will not know that camouflage took place until the truth is revealed sometime later. The agent can mask the facts so that the target can honestly find it hard to learn by chance about the deception.

2. **Disguise:** This is another component of the deception process. It occurs when the agent depicts themselves as other people to the subject. The agent can decide to hides something from the subject, such as their real name, what they do for a living, with whom they were with, and what they are up to when they are out. This is more than simply changing the suit someone wears in a piece of film; the agent tries to change their entire personality to deceive their target. Some examples demonstrate the use of disguise in the deception process. One is to dress in interactions with the agent, sometimes as someone else, so that they cannot be identified or recognized. The agent will do this to get back into a multitude of people who don't like them, change their personality to make people like them, or otherwise advance their goals. In some situations, the word disguise can be referred to when the agent disguises the true nature of a proposal in the hope that it hides any controversial effect or motive for such a proposal.

3. **Simulation:** This is the third component of deception. The agent shows the untrue subject information. There are three important techniques that an agent can use in simulation:

a. The first is **mimicry**, where the agent is unknowingly depicting something similar to themselves. They could be talking about someone else's idea and give credit to themselves by saying that the idea is theirs.
b. **Fabrication** is the second technique where an agent will use something in reality and change it so that it becomes different. They can tell a story and add embellishments to make the story sound better or worse than it was. While the main story may have happened, it is going to have things added on top of it and change the whole narrative.
c. Lastly, we have a **distraction** as a form of simulation. This is when the agent tries to make the subject concentrate on something other than the facts, usually baiting or proposing something more appealing than the reality of the matter. For example, when the husband is having an affair and feels that the wife is starting to learn about it, he may take a diamond ring home to confuse her. The problem with this strategy is that it does not always last long, and the agent must find another way to confuse the subject to continue the process.

## How to Use Deception

Psychological research is the sector that mostly uses deception as it is necessary to determine the actual results. The explanation behind this deception says that people are very sensitive to the way they look both to others and themselves and that their self-awareness can distort or interfere with the way the subject is compared to doing research, in normal circumstances, in which they do not feel examined. The deception is intended to make people feel more comfortable so that the agent can get the right results.

The agent may be interested, for example, in knowing which circumstances a student could cheat on a test. If the agent specifically investigates the student, the subjects are unlikely to confess to lying, and the agent could not make out who tells the truth and who does not. In this scenario, the agent should use a distraction to get a clear picture of how cheating fraud takes place. Alternatively, the agent could suggest that the study is about how intuitive the subject is; even in the process, you can say that you can look at the answers of someone else before offering your answers. This analysis includes the conclusion.

Alternatively, the researcher may suggest that the research seeks to find out how insightful the subject is. The subject may even be advised that they have the opportunity to look for answers from someone else before providing their answers. Once concluded the deception experiment the agent should ask the subject what the real nature of the trial is and why the deception is required. In addition, some agents will also give a quick description of the results between all participants when the study is carried out.

## How to Detect Deception

If the subject wants to stop deceit in their life so that the mind games that follow can be stopped, it is often a good idea to learn how to detect deception when it occurs. It is often hard for the subject to decide that deception exists unless the agent slips up and either tells a simple or flat lie or contradicts something which is already real. Although it may be difficult for the agent to deceive the subject for a while, it is often the case among people who know one another. It is often very hard to detect if deception occurs because no signs are present.

Deception, however, can put a great deal of pressure on the mental workings of the agent because they need to find out how to recall all the comments, they have made on the subject so that the tale remains plausible and consistent. One mistake on the part of the agent and the subject will tell something is wrong. The agent is more likely to redirect information to tip off the subject, either via non-verbal or verbal signals, because of the pressure they have to keep the past straight. Researchers believe that identification of deception is a mental, dynamic, and complex process that often differs from the message being exchanged. The Interpersonal Deceit Theory shows that deception is an iterative and complex mechanism of control that exists between the agent who manipulates information in such a way as to make it different from the reality and the subject who then tries to find out whether the message is true or not. The acts of the agent shall be linked with the actions of the subject after the message is received. The agent must disclose non-verbal and verbal details during this exchange, which will lead the subject to deceit. The subject might be able to tell at some points that the agent has been lying to them.

# Conclusion

This book examined dark psychology and the use of different techniques that can be used to manipulate people. It is becoming more and more prevalent in our society. This book also examined how you can prevent being manipulated, including steps you can take if someone is trying to manipulate you.

A person who is suffering from these dark psychology traits will not hesitate to use trickery, lies, or deceit to achieve their goals. When they are successful and finally get what they want, they will show no remorse for the people they have manipulated. Most of the time these people may even feel justified and believe that what they did was okay. Those that are manipulated by such a person may not even know what is going on. Instead of seeing the person for who they are, they might mistake the manipulator as someone with good intentions.

Dark psychology has no boundaries. These tactics may be used by a young person to get what they want or they may be employed by someone much older and more experienced in manipulating others.

To give the manipulator the upper hand, it is common for them to disguise their efforts as something else entirely. Rather than admitting that they are using someone else, they may claim to be doing something nice for them. However, this is just a ploy to get what they want.

This form of manipulation cannot be stopped by being aware of it, as the manipulator will find a way to convince their intended victim that it is all in good fun or something else entirely. Laws have been designed to help prevent this form of manipulation, but they do not always work as planned.

What are the signs that you might be a victim of dark psychology? Do you feel that someone is using you? It is important to figure out quickly how someone is using you and to do everything possible to avoid being manipulated. Learning to spot the signs of manipulation is an important part of overcoming this negative form of influence.

One sign that you could be the victim of dark psychology is when you feel like someone may be using your emotions to get what they want. This may come in the form of friendship or even love, but it can be difficult to tell when someone is doing this. Again, just because you are aware of someone using your emotions does not mean that they are doing it on purpose. A manipulator will use any means to get what they want, even if this means using your emotions to do so.

Another sign that you could be the victim of dark psychology is when someone is playing with your mind. There are many ways that someone can play with your mind to get what they want, and this is an effective way to manipulate their victim. You may have heard of the term "mind games" or even "emotional games", and these are just different names for what dark psychology is all about.

One of the most common ways that someone will play with your mind is through manipulation. They may claim to be doing something nice for you, but this might not be true at all. Instead, they may be using you to get what they want. This could come in the form of attention, or it could come in the form of a free meal or even a gift.

The main thing to watch out for when you are around someone that uses dark psychology is their intentions. If someone is doing nice things for you but this is not because they care about you or want to help, then there is a good chance that they have an ulterior motive.

As you can see, being manipulated with dark psychology is a serious thing. While it may not be possible to avoid everything in life, you do have the ability to try and overcome this negative form of influence. By learning about it and watching for the signs that someone may be using you, you will be able to overcome this problem more easily.

The most common method of using hypnosis and brainwashing has been through cults. While there seems to be no broad consensus on the definition of a cult, most authors agree that cults are small groups that can be easily controlled and kept separate from outside influences and that their teachings may be in opposition to the views held by the rest of society.

Cults are known to follow certain patterns related to hypnosis and brainwashing. For example, while concentration and meditation are part of the routine of cult leaders, they also commonly use isolation to keep their followers away from the rest of society. Since many cult leaders tend to have a charismatic personality, followers often feel special or privileged just for being accepted by them. This is accomplished through processes that tend to isolate the followers, while at the same time, they are forced to rely on the leaders for scarce resources such as food and clothes. This results in deep psychological dependence on the leaders and leaves them unable to make decisions without their approval and support. In this way, cults can be seen as a transition from segregation or isolation to imprisonment.

Some authors have also described a process of brainwashing as a three-stage cycle: an indoctrination stage, where the followers are educated about the cult; an isolation stage, where followers are exposed to psychological pressure and deprived of their identity; and an indoctrination stage that reinforces the original teachings given in the first part. The tendency of cults to use brainwashing techniques is evident in the way they are created. In most cases, cults can be attributed to a charismatic individual who has implemented basic techniques of hypnosis or mind control to attract followers. Then, through social interactions and rituals that pressure people into submission, they seem to convert their followers from a normal state into an abnormal state where they are completely dependent on the leader. Whether it is done through hypnosis or mind control, the effect is the same, and there seems to be a strong relationship between mind-altering techniques and cult creation.

# Book 2: DARK PSYCHOLOGY

# Introduction

The human body operates like a computer, constantly processing information and giving out information in the form of body language. We all understand what it is, but most of us do not know exactly how it works.

That is because, without our conscious awareness, the process of obtaining and decoding non-verbal communication is often completed. It is just true. Human beings are genetically programmed to scan and quickly understand their significance for facial and behavioral signals. We see somebody's movement and determine the meaning of that gesture automatically.

And for a long, long time we have been doing this. As a culture, we knew how to win friends and influence people long before that we learned how to use words or avoid/place/confront people with whom we could not be friends. Our ancestors made decisions on survival based solely on complex bits of visual information that they obtained from others. And they've done that early. Throughout our prehistory, it was often a matter of life or death to decide quickly whether a circumstance or individual was risky.

Almost all of us can read body language, yet its rules may seem mysterious, and at one point, we all let our bodies say things we did not want. Even without being aware of it, you are going to know that sometimes a meeting or transaction is going very well, and sometimes it goes even without changing a lot about your conversation. The explanation for this is in the culture of the body that you or they used. You said the right thing with your face and the reciprocated person with a positive atmosphere or, on the other hand, you might have had a rough day, and another person could only read your anger from the way you stood.

Flimsy body language may cause real problems for many of us, sometimes we may seem upset when we are not, sometimes people may not take us seriously, or they may feel we are insincere. In many situations, fake body language is also important, at one time or another we have to sell something (whether it is thoughts, ideas, or used cars), and we are not going to believe in what we sell. Nevertheless, we need to say that we are doing our body language. Luckily, you can change the way you use body language, and just be mindful of what hand gesture means and what your eyebrow twitch can say, you can start saying what you mean in both your words and your body.

This book will help you to achieve a good working knowledge of body language, how to analyze people, and how to subtly use body language to manipulate people, with or without their consent.

Consider these 2 near-identical scenarios; both start with you sitting at your favorite restaurant table, it is a busy night, and you luckily got there just in time to avoid having to tip the busboy to skip the queue. You are on the tail end of your main course in deep conversation with your buddy about ordering dessert or not. It is a night of pleasure; why not? So, the waitress comes here; she looks down at your table and asks, "Are you finished?"

- **Scenario 1:** With her hands on her hips, she asks this question, stood up straight, her lips slightly pursed, and she speaks quickly without waiting to see if you were ready to answer.
- **Scenario 2:** She is bent over slightly to make better eye contact, she is waiting for you to finish speaking before answering, her hands are waiting by her side, or maybe even giving your shoulder a gentle brush, and she is asking her voice with a soft inflection because it is a question and not a sarcastic motion.

Through experience and just reading these 2 fictional stories, you can see what was going on and what these 2 waitresses were saying with their bodies. In the case, one of the somewhat villainous waitresses was saying, "hurry up because someone else needs this seat." She wanted you to quit in the second scenario, but she did not want you to feel under pressure. After all, you might still want dessert.

Body language is how we interact with our bodies in a non-verbal manner. This description may be deceptive because, generally speaking, body language is not considered to include open hand movements such as raising a thumb or fingers or using sign language—these kinds of body gestures are still verbal and explicit in some type of way. Body language is commonly regarded as the subtle accidental and implicit ways of interacting with our body; even just a middle finger can be viewed as playful, given the right kind of grimace. In reality, in the same domain as body language, even some verbal communicating is considered because how we make comments is just as essential as what we do to show what we mean. There, of course, there is a middle ground—pointing the finger is a clear form of interaction. Still, it can also be automatic, and finding out what our hands are doing is certainly central to understanding the language of the body.

Body language is the analysis of our facial expressions, gestures, mannerisms, and how we move around to decide how to translate what we say, and sometimes when we do not speak, to understand what a person might think or feel. It is good not to be anxious at an interview in your voice, but if you are sweating like you are going through a tough time, people already know you are putting it on.

The question of whether body language is deliberate or accidental is a very difficult question to answer. There are only a few rare occasions to ruminate or witness what is happening not just in the conversation, but what is happening outside and around you, reactions occur almost naturally. You will often find yourself thinking, "that was not what I intended to say," and in those situations, you may start deconstructing your thoughts to sort out what you thought at the time.

Their body language seems to have even less feedback from their brains than this, which has culminated in some thinking about a conscious and subconscious brain. This kind of separation is useful to many motivational speakers because it is dramatic and simplistic; the body seems to be working on its behalf, exposing your inner urges—it would be some sort of hidden secret to commanding. The truth is that this division is typically filled with Freudian psychology leftovers that are no longer taken with a lot of integrity.

For simplicity's sake, it is best to think of the brain as having the parts you are paying attention to at the moment, and next to that there is a lot of background details and systems working behind the scenes, but you can easily concentrate on them and change them at your own will. The way a machine works is a perfect analogy; you can normally run just a few programs at a time. Some people would like you to believe that while you are busy, your old emails and Solitaire plot something against you, but that is not the case. Body language functions as part of your conscious mind, as all you are doing at the moment does, but it also operates on some instinctual levels and mechanisms that we do not fully understand-just yet! We also hear deliberations about how much of our interaction depends on body language; some figures suggest that 55% of what we say is in the regions around our nose and eyes (one famous figure indicates that only 7% of communication is speech). While these statistics vary greatly from source to source, and it is not always clear what these numbers mean, even in real terms, it is sufficient to know that a significant amount of daily communication is almost impossible without some form of NVC (non-verbal communication). Remember how we interact through text messages or online chat systems since so much of what we write can seem deceptive or angry without a mouth or face behind it, it can almost seem appropriate to use smiley faces and emoticons. A simple question like, "Come to the dinner party?" Without a polite smile next to it, it can sound accusatory. Note also how what we say is completely context-related, it is difficult even to think of a word that can be said outside a situation. Take a simple word like "thank you," it could be interpreted as sarcastic, disingenuous, friendly, or if followed by a hug or tears, it could be viewed as something highly sincere.

# Chapter 1: How to Analyze People

At the point when you figure out how to peruse individuals, you'll understand that it's an essential ability in your own and business life. Regardless of whether you are gaining practical experience in companionship, vocation, nurturing, or sentiment, figuring out how to check individuals offers you an opportunity to create important bits of knowledge and assemble sound determinations. Some would say there's no quick method to discover concerning understanding people. This is valid. The learning may take a dash of time; anyway, after training, you will want to rapidly contemplate someone and get an awesome vibe of who they're and what they wish. When you pay time figuring out how to get others, you'll see yourself higher. You should initially see the dividers that individuals develop and the hindrances you have put in your manner. At the point when people uncover themselves to other people, the truth just includes light-weight in layers. The underlying layer is that the layer people show to you when you're an outsider. They could be sitting with you at a bus station or in another environmental factor. Subjects exemplify recent developments and subsequently the climate — guiltless themes that way. Most people are cozy talking about them. The subsequent layer is that the one individual shows once they feel good with you. Collaborators may talk with you about themselves a great deal if they capture you a touch. They may talk concerning their musings in regards to feelings concerning elective wide subjects. The third close-to-home layer is kept available later for those who have personal connections with you. This incorporates mates and shut companions. These set aside a ton of effort to create, and trust is acquired as that point passes. The profundity of what's uncovered is greater than the other 2 layers. Your feelings of trepidation, objectives and personal issues fall in this layer. The deepest, fourth layer is that the piece of individuals that they don't impart to anybody. It contains their haziest, most profound insider facts and considerations, and some of these they would support not to recognize. They probably won't even have re-visitation of terms by the by for certain subjects in this layer. This is the reason they are awkward offering these things to anybody. To peruse others, you need to traverse their layers. You don't need to go all the way to the personal level; indeed, anyway, the farther in your entrance is, the extra dependable your perusing will be. To understand people, you need likewise to eliminate the hindrances you place among yourself and others. These boundaries are your projections and your biases. Projections are your inclination (and that of every other person) to close your psyche and eyes to something upsetting or awkward. You will project your read onto things since it makes them simpler with which to bargain. Biases don't straightforwardly talk over with just racial bias. This can be a small 50% of it; it isn't the whole half. Each time you make a closely-held conviction, negative or positive, without inspecting current realities, you are biased.

## Why Analyze People

Holding thoughts essentially dependent on the political arrangement, shading, race, or even what people wear mists your understanding capacity. Your biases might be founded for the most part on your childhood, your apprehensions, or various elective things. To peruse people viably, you should be unbiased, which implies that having void hands. You might need to defeat your projections and biases as well to be level-headed. Show restraint. Fill your hands gradually with information, in this way that your decisions are not hurried. Try not to be in this manner eager that you simply miss the gigantic picture. Permit film to completely grow, along these lines that you don't get humiliated or disillusioned.

This is regularly what perusing individuals resemble. Learning the correct procedures to decipher individuals can help you fight the temptation to jump to hurried ends. Hold off before you make an ultimate conclusion concerning people. On the fundamental components of your life, it's crucial to handle whether people reveal the truth or mislead you in business or individual fields. Tragically, individuals are not, more often than not, excellent when it includes identifying lies. A character inclines to accept others, and for associations where little is in question, this functions as great as. While you can't analyze each cooperation, you have misleading signs; there are some clear manners by which to peruse people, see them more, and work out if they are coming clean or not. There are times when you wish to know whether you are accepting the story straight.

- When necessary, arrangements rely upon you, it's imperative to comprehend what people advise you—verbally and something else. It is likewise valuable to comprehend when people have an example of lying or being honest.
- Precisely perusing people isn't a present; rather, it's an ability that you can dominate if you concentrate on the correct pointers. The requirement for trust greases up almost every part of our lives, from individual to gifted.
- Perusing people precisely is an indispensable portion of knowing truth from lies. They are stronger to identify on the off chance that falsehoods are told on TV or a site. If you become a decent people peruse, they cannot so effectively fool you when you are vis-à-vis the situation.
- It's ordinarily simpler to shape your decisions than to depend on others to realize who is deceiving you and who is coming clean.
- Clinicians who have contemplated duplicity caution that there is not a secure way to peruse individuals. You'll turn out to be very precise if you apply, however. You won't perpetually be utilizing your people-perusing abilities to identify double-dealing. Any way this can be one in everything about most normal things to notice.

- Lying isn't one strategy with social pointers that are always unmistakable. On the off chance that liars don't mind concerning the truth, they are hard to peruse. However, if you figure out how to peruse perspiring, squirming, and various practices, these can now and again—yet not generally—demonstrate double-dealing.
- They may likewise mean the individual is restless. Specialists and criminal investigators utilize numerous stunts of cross-examination that you'll have the option to receive to support your chances of recognizing trickiness.
- You will figure out how to focus and appearance at anxious signs and give closer consideration to what people say. People who are acceptable at deluding others may have sharpened their abilities well, and they won't be difficult to get inside the demonstration. Hoodlums improve at lying a ton normally; they are cross-examined.

However, we tend to don't have any desire to stress concerning criminal geniuses after examining them for most people. You ought to try and be prepared for lying yourself. It's common to accept people and to dodge the truth, particularly if it's excruciating. This makes it simpler for individuals who misdirect. When you have the option to peruse the signs that are never-ending present, you'll have the option to get what "tells" you need and comprehend those methods for specific motions. There is no 100% sure technique to see someone's opinion, any way you can peruse individuals precisely up to 80% or subsequently if you dominate at it.

## Ways to Learn How to Analyze People

It could be the hardest portion of figuring out how to peruse others. It would help if you saw yourself starting. Remember your emotions and see why you are the methodology you are. Everyone is entirely unexpected. Anyway, we tend to all have similitudes, as well.

- It is normal for individuals to move their bodies while they talk. Honest discourse may exemplify pushing ahead and reclining. A few groups are firm once they talk; anyway, liars will, in general, freeze their movements to try not to release any signals that might be emotive. As a ready "people peruse," you'll notice that an absence of body movement is an indication of misleading.
- Shoulders say a store in regards to the individual talking. They drop when the speaker is exasperated and hunch up when they're awkward. Shrugs may signify "I

couldn't care less" or "I don't secure." Incomplete shrugs will show an attempt at trickery. Hands are appallingly expressive body parts.

- When you talk with someone, notice their "artists," which implies that they utilize their hands to pressure and emphasize discourse. Anticipate people who adorn their narrating or who don't utilize their hands in discourse.
- These can be signs that they're not put resources into what they say. Furthermore, anticipate unnatural developments, as collapsed palms or grasped clenched hands. They are pointers that the speakers are limiting themselves from saying a certain something.
- Watch the arms when somebody is talking, as well. Underuse will show unscrupulousness. The intersection of the arms is guarded, and at times people even lock them in that position.
- A place of open arms with palms out is an open, legitimate position; crossed arms demonstrate a shut position.
- When you're addressing somebody, what's in the individual's temperament? Do they have all the earmarks of being curious about everyone's benefit? Or then again, would they say they are a ton of normally negative?
- Negative people commonly need something. On the off chance that wants aren't met, people respond contrarily for the most part. Is the individual you are addressing a hermit, or will they favor a group? They are altogether likely OK with those people to explain the off chance that they prefer swarms—they make them think like manner.
- It's normal to cherish people that are more similar to you. If the individual with whom you're talking spends time with totally various kinds of people, at that point, they're presumably liberal. Most receptive individuals are compassionate and care concerning others.

A few people normally search internally and don't care for swarms. This proposes that they ordinarily don't feel they might want an amicable arrangement of relationships with various people. They may feel that they don't have a place in a very bunch, or they'll have social apprehensions. On the off chance that an individual will know things uniquely compared to other people, maybe their way of life is not the same as the one you live in. When you understand people, you need to focus on where they're from. Hence, you essentially comprehend their conventional practices. There are reasons why individuals get things done. Discover those reasons. Feel liberal to ask people for what good reason they are doing something, yet not in a scornful strategy. On the off chance that they answer, you'll secure a great deal of respect for them.

Notice their flaws without judging. At the point when you filter individuals, keep your psyche open. Everybody has shortcomings and flaws. Rapidly examining somebody's appearance once you meet the first run-through might disclose to you a smidgen more about them. Some of this can be cunning. However, you must do a sweep, not simply notice a couple of parts of their look. Are their articles of clothing custom-made? They altogether likelihood has money if they are. This isn't acceptable or undesirable; it's simply a perception. Is their hair wet? They're most probable a bustling one that just bounced out of the shower and went to work. Is this eternity precise? No, anyway, a few times it is.

# Chapter 2: How to Read People

Mind-reading is essentially knowing what other people truly mean without them saying it out loud, or even despite them stating otherwise. Anyone has the potential ability to analyze others, with the right set of skills and training. It is, however, time-consuming and requires focus and patience. An open-minded approach cannot be overstated. The reader needs to be completely receptive to the subject's thoughts and nuances, far removed from any prejudices that they may have about the matter at hand or the environment in which the reading is taking place.

Particular attention should be paid to the subject's eyes, as they are said to be the window to the soul. A person's general personality should be noted too, which includes but is not limited to appearance, overall behavior, physical movements, and, not surprisingly, the gut feeling you have about them. Listening to your intuition can be valuable with such matters.

## Context

There are many reasons to want to read someone's mind. Empathy is the most common reason because we long for a close connection with other people. Humans are social beings and this need is nature.

Most of the basic emotions, sadness, joy, fear, anger, surprise, and disgust are expressed in the same way across all cultures and races. This makes it easy to read said emotions in another person. The subtle nuances are what is much harder to decipher, and it takes a dedicated person to learn how to interpret each person correctly.

We all seek ease when it comes to communicating with others. Reading someone's mind can help adjust how we react to any given situation. Relating also makes it possible to respond suitably.

This skill may also aid in lie detection. Being able to look past words to ascertain the truth is a valuable ability. This is most useful in criminology and law enforcement professions, where it is essential to know when and what information a perpetrator may be withholding. For example, a suspect who has an accomplice may not want to give them up. A terrorist with a bomb hidden somewhere may not want to reveal the location of the incendiary device. It is, therefore, necessary to have such analytical skills, which to decipher the information that may not necessarily be spoken. Speed and accuracy are imperative in these instances.

The situation or the environment in which a non-verbal cue applies matters. The same thing done in a different setting or as a reaction to various circumstances could mean other things. For example, a cough in a draughty room could be just that, an innocent cough, whereas a cough after an especially awkward comment could be a sign of discomfort.

One should always be careful not to pay mind to stereotypes as a mind reader. People and their body language are as diverse as the fish in the sea. One person's "tell" may not necessarily be another's. This is well evidenced by high stakes poker players who take time and resources to research their opponents and figure out what their weakness is, to gain a competitive edge.

## Considering More Than One Sign

Communication is done through multiple distinct channels; there are verbal, non-verbal, written, and visual. These are all used differently, according to the message one wants to put across. For example, someone who is angry at someone else may text or write to them in capital letters to express their anger, which would be equated to shouting if the person re actually speaking their thoughts. It is essential to understand the subject's thought process and how it applies to all these.

More often than not, it takes a combination of signs to bring the intended message out clearly. A mind reader needs to learn by constant practice how to correctly interpret a combination of signs in the subject. For example, eyes downcast could mean that someone is ashamed. The same motion while continually looking outside or away from you may mean that they have something to hide, or that they are not interested in the current topic of conversation.

Signs are also vital because, for someone who may be living with one kind of challenge or another, they may need more than one way to understand a statement or concept. Likewise, they will also communicate with more than one sense. Examples include people with failing vision, the hearing impaired, and even people within the autism spectrum, especially those who may not necessarily understand typical social cues and need help interpreting them.

## Not Knowing the Person

Reading a person unknown to you can pose a challenge, but it is still possible. Meeting someone for the first time is a whole new experience that registers as a "new file" in the brain and sets the tone for consecutive meetings. Hence the adage "first impressions are very important."

Reading a stranger's mind may require more patience and more intense focus, so as not to miss out on subtle cues. One should be careful not to make the subject uncomfortable, though, and it is recommended not to stare for too long. An initial 15 seconds should be enough to get a general understanding of someone without making them uneasy.

A short series of basic questions, like name and address, should elicit truthful answers. These inquiries can help establish a baseline for that person's facial expressions, tone of voice, and eye contact when they are telling the truth. Another generally accepted "tell" is the firmness of one's handshake. A firm handshake may denote confidence, while a weak handshake may denote a non-committal attitude.

One should also consider other factors that could determine a person's responses. These include age and cultural background. For example, someone born in the 40s or 50s may be more conservative on subjects to do with sexuality or religion than a millennial might be. Also, in some cultures, handshakes are not appropriate, especially between individuals of different genders. Being unaware of such a seemingly trivial matter could lead one to misread a subject who does not want a handshake or who gives only a fleeting one.

When reading a stranger, it is best not to make assumptions. Such haste can lead to misunderstandings. Take the time to learn the basics of an individual. A current mood may not be that person's usual disposition. For example, maybe they had a hard time finding parking and seem flustered, which is just a momentary state. Their real character should be evident once the agitation is over.

## Biases

We should also be particularly careful about applying our judgments and perceptions to the person whose mind is being read. These are referred to as cognitive biases. On the contrary, we should consciously strive to observe or listen to the other individual objectively and rationally.

Understanding these biases helps us to avoid the pitfalls of misunderstanding or wrongly interpreting the other person's responses or intended meaning. Being objective toward others is also a wise way to conduct oneself, in general. These preconceived notions are the halo effect, the confirmation bias, the actor-observer bias, the false consensus effect, and the anchoring bias.

# The Halo Effect

Is also referred to as "the physical attractiveness stereotype." It is the tendency to let our initial impression of a person influence what we think of them overall. It has the potential to cloud our vision of the person's other characteristics just because we judged them at first sight. The more physically appealing one is to us, the more favorably we are disposed to them, and vice versa, without taking into consideration the person's other character traits.

For example, a well-dressed person on the street would gain more of our attention and possibly admiration than a is shabbily dressed person, yet the well-dressed person may be a ruthless grifter who preys on retirees while the shabbily dressed one could be an honest person down on their luck. This is also very much evidenced at job interviews, where one is encouraged to attend well-groomed to give a positive first impression. We associate attractiveness with benevolence.

# The Confirmation Bias

Is when people lean towards information that seems to confirm formerly held beliefs. It is a polarizing pitfall. People may listen to the same story but only pick from it what confirms their opinions, to the exclusion of all others. For example, a presidential campaign usually has supporters and opponents, and whatever a candidate says or does is sure to be interpreted to suit either side. It will be praised and touted by supporters, while the same action will be vilified and discredited by opponents. We should be careful not to let our long-standing ideals determine what we hear and understand from the person whose mind we are reading. Instead, we should listen logically and rationally to reach an informed conclusion.

# The Actor Observer Bias

Is when we perceive others and attribute their actions to several variables, influenced by whether we are the actor or the observer in a situation. That is, when it comes to our actions, we are more likely to explain ourselves by attributing faults to external influences while blaming other people's actions for their internal causes. For example, imagine being late to a meeting and saying the traffic was unbearable yet blaming another person who comes in a few minutes later by saying that they are just lazy. This kind of bias should be far from a mind reader's modus operandi. Otherwise, the exercise would only be clouded with endless blame games.

## The False Consensus Effect

This refers to our tendency to overestimate how much other people agree with our own beliefs, behaviors, attitudes, and values. It stems from the fact that we spend most of our time with the same people, who tend to share our opinions. This leads us to believe that our thoughts are the same as the majority, even outside of our circle. Those who think like us are good and normal, while everything else is not. This is a dangerous attitude for anyone because it can easily foster intolerance.

Thinking this way limits our understanding of the subject's opinion if it differs from our own. For example, a spirited defense of the benefits of eating meat or animal protein may be unacceptable or repulsive to a vegan, who would thereby miss the subtle nuances of how the other is expresses sincerity and conviction. We must remember that the world is full of people from different backgrounds.

## The Anchoring Bias

This occurs when we allow ourselves to be overly influenced by the first piece of information that we hear regarding any subject. This is a tricky cognitive device because it has a significant bearing on how a conversation or negotiation will proceed. For example, imagine hearing that "there is Ebola in Africa." This is a blanket statement, as Africa is a continent, not a single country, and the disease may be confined to only one country or one region, and the rest of the continent is Ebola-free.

An over-cautious European government may issue a travel advisory to Africa, thereby affecting many other countries who are reliant on tourism, Ebola-free though, they may be. It also affects serious matters like medicine. A doctor can create an anchoring point, where their first impression of the symptoms a patient may present could lead to them giving a wrong diagnosis.

# Chapter 3: The Eyes, Mirror of the Soul

The eyes are said to be the windows to our soul and our thoughts. There is so much that you can tell just by looking at a person's eyes and the various movements that they make. To be a stellar analyzer, follow the steps below:

## 1. Establish Your Reason for Wanting to Analyze Someone

Do you want to know whether they are lying to you or are you trying to validate their authenticity? It doesn't matter if you are dealing with a stranger or not. The rules are the same.

## 2. Baseline the Eyes

The baseline process involves establishing how a person's eyes behave in a normal and non-threatening situation. Do this by asking about casual and neutral topics such as what they think about the weather, what they would like to drink, as well as movie and hobby preferences. The baselining questions should be no-brainers and something that nobody would lie about. Take note of how the eyes behave as you are having this talk, and you have your baseline.

## 3. Look For Any Signs of Eye Deviation From the Baseline

For instance, if you are on a first date, keep tabs on the conversations and topics that make the other party's eyes deviate from the baseline. These are potential red flags, and you may want to dig a little deeper. Psychologists and the FBI use this tactic all the time, and they can establish which questions they need to dig deeper on.
Baseline deviations can take the form of:

### 1. Eye Blocking

Eye blocking often happens when a person feels threatened, or when they are repulsed by something they see or hear. This is an indication of a very uncomfortable situation, mostly due to disbelief or innate disagreement. Some people display eye blocking by rapid blinking while others take to rubbing the eyes. Learning to read eye-blocking can help you realize when you have repulsed people, enabling you to make it up or change the topic immediately.

Many years ago, I was out on a date with a person that I liked and felt instant chemistry with. As we got to know each other, I said something demeaning about people who opted for a divorce rather than staying and fighting for their marriage. I was trying to come off as a keeper, and I missed his sudden change of demeanor, which involved a lot of eye rubbing. Turns out he had married young and had already been divorced once. Needless to say, we never went out for a second date. If I had known what I know now, I could have potentially saved the situation.

## 2. Squinting

People will often squint if they do not like you or something that you are saying. This behavior is similar to eye-blocking, and you should address it quickly or clarify whatever it is that you have said before it gets worse.

## 3. Eye Positions

Understanding eye positions is immensely important in the analysis process, and it will tell you a lot with minimum effort.

You can analyze these eye movements when doing cross-examinations, interviews, or generally when a person is talking to you. From this analysis, you can tell whether a person is lying to you or not.

Right eye movements are associated with truth, while left eye movements are associated with lies/making things up. You must realize that human beings will always have a strong desire to be liked and accepted, and sometimes creating a facade of who they want to seem like the best option. Regardless of the content through which you are analyzing a person, knowing this technique will help you know who you are dealing with.

When a person is talking about a past event, they often rely on stored memories that they can vividly remember and describe. The memories are said to be on the left side of the brain, and that is why eye movements are to their upper left (your right if you are directly facing them). However, if a person is just being deceptive and has to come up with a fake story, the eyes will shift to your left. The same applies when they are talking about remembered sounds such as conversations they claim to have had in the past.

When a person is having an internal dialogue/debate, they will most likely glance toward the lower left. However, remembering a feeling will have them glancing toward the lower right

Movement of the eyes is considered to be one of the most accurate methods of analyzing a person/situation, although it is not foolproof. You have to pay very close attention to the movements and put them in the context of the conversation to avoid making wrong judgments. In most cases, you have to associate the movement with the exact word or sentence that a person is saying. Consider the following scenario:

A person may be telling the truth about an incident and add bits of lies in between. For example, a statement like "I graduated in business and commerce from Harvard University" may have two parts. It may be true that indeed the person graduated in business and commerce, with the only exception being that they did not attend Harvard. If you are keen enough, you may notice the sudden shift in eye movements which will be red flags. If you are not sure about what you have observed, it is prudent to ask follow-up questions. For example, you can ask the person to tell you all about Harvard and what their experience was in the institution. Such a question requires a lengthy answer, and you will be able to observe eye movements much more accurately at this point.

## 4. Sideways Glances

When a person is giving sideways glances, it is often an indication that they are uncertain, and often an indication of nervousness. You may want to ask follow-up questions since this may be a sign of deception. Again, it depends on the context of the conversation since most people are prone to making sideways glances when they are withholding certain information. Maybe they just don't trust you.

In most cases, you will only make credible inferences when you understand what all the eye movements mean and connect them to the context of the conversation. Remember, if you are not sure, the best thing to do is to ask more follow-up questions and analyze more signs.

# Chapter 4: How Our Body Speaks

Body language involves how we use our physical behavior, expressions, and manners to reveal non-verbal information about ourselves, which is usually done unconsciously. Many people are not aware of it, but in all your interactions, you are constantly giving out body cues and wordless signals that serve either to reinforce/solidify the interaction or to contradict what you are trying to say.
Your entire non-verbal behaviors transmit a loud and strong message that continues even after you stop talking. There are instances when what someone says might differ from what their body language is communicating. Hence, in this case, it will be easy for the person you are interacting with to pass you off as a liar. If someone asked for a favor and gave a frown after giving a no, you have ended up confusing the person. With this kind of mixed-signal, the person might be confused about what to believe. However, if the person understands the concept of body language, they would probably just walk away since the body language is unconscious and gives someone out by revealing true intention.

## Positive Body Language

A positive body language is welcoming, attractive, and full of confidence. Here are some body language cues that signal positivity:

### Smile

A genuine, real, and appropriate smile carries a lot of power. It lifts the mood and is welcoming. It makes people feel better and lightens up the atmosphere. It is surely attractive as well. You have been eyeing a lady and stealing glances at her. Suddenly you made eye contact, and she smiled. That is a cue for you to know that you are accepted.

### Eye Contact

I sometimes remember a rift I had with my girlfriend. In a bid to resolve it, we had a face-to-face conversation. Throughout the conversation, she avoided my gaze. This was understandable and expected as she was mad at me. However, what I tried to do was get her to make eye contact with me. Eye contact creates some form of connection between 2 people. This is how important eye contact is.

Talking with someone and looking them in the eye makes them feel important and valued. This is because eye contact signifies attention. If you are with somebody and the person keeps glancing around or looking at their watch or their phone, it is a sure sign of a lack of interest in the interaction.

### The Right Posture

The posture of the person you are interacting with also carries a lot of meaning. A person standing or sitting straight, for instance, sends a positive message. This is different from a slouch, tensed, or unrelaxed posture. Someone who looks confident and relaxed will surely attract others to them.
In any interaction, pay attention to where the person leans. A person who leans toward you is interested in the interaction and subject of conversation.
The head direction matters as well. A slight move of the head is a positive indication that the other party is curious and interested in the conversation.

### The Right Touch

Touching makes people feel good as it releases endorphins. It should, however, be used appropriately and in the right context. A firm and warm handshake, for instance, indicates that you are accepted. The same is true with a pat on the shoulder. A pat on the shoulder from your boss, for instance, is an indication that you have scored some good points.

### The Direction of the Body

Pay attention to the direction the other person's body is facing. This signals whether you have their attention or not. A body or feet angled away gives the impression that the person wants to go away.

### Personal Space

The distance and space between people are an indication of the level of relation between them. People nearby say 2-4 feet are close friends or in a relationship. While a distance of about four to ten feet is for social interaction between people you are not very familiar with.

### Nodding

Pay attention to the rate and frequency of nodding. A slow nod is a sign that someone is paying attention to you and is interested in the conversation.

### Mirroring

When a person is copying your body language, vocal speech, gestures, or body movement pattern, there is a big chance you have established rapport.

## Negative Body Language

There are negative body signals that show discomfort, hostility, anxiety, or a pure lack of interest. Pay attention to the following:

### Tense

A tense person is uncomfortable, which could be because of many things. You might have said something that turned them off, or perhaps you are standing too close to them. And better still, it could have nothing to do with you.

### Fast Anxious Movements

If you are uncomfortable, the body is programmed to trigger you to flee the environment and situation. Hence, the pattern of speech, rate of movement, etc. of the other person indicates they are uncomfortable with you.

### Desperately Trying to Be Still

Think about it. In a normal, relaxed setting, you are free. You move any part of your body unconsciously and without any resistance since there is nothing to worry about. However, watch out if the person sits still or is not gesticulating, especially if this is something they would normally do. It could point out nervousness and discomfort that they are desperately trying to hide.

## Lack of Eye Contact

If you are interested in something, your eyes will be fixed on that thing. It's not necessarily fixed, but much of your gaze will be directed at that thing. Hence, pay attention to the eyes of the person you are with. Looking away, lack of eye contact, looking at the floor, or glancing at the watch are all negative body signals that show a lack of interest in the interaction.

## Crossed Arms and Legs

While crossed arms and legs are a sign of defensiveness, they could also mean that the person feels cold, or perhaps they just find this position comfortable. However, it could also be that the person you are with is not interested in the interaction.
The same thing applies to cross the legs. Watch out for legs crossed with the knees pointing toward you. It is a pure negative sign.
These are the classic sign of closed body language. Also, pay attention to where the other person is facing. Is it toward or away from you?

## Body Pointing Away From You

Give attention to the direction in which the torso, feet, and overall body are pointing. If any of this is away from you, the person has lost interest in the interaction. You might or might not be the cause of this body signal. For instance, in a board meeting, someone who keeps glancing at the door with the legs pointed toward the exit is bored and wants to leave.

## Position of the Arms

Arms in the pocket or hands clasped in front of you, give an impression that something is wrong.

## Slouching

Your posture could also give out a positive or negative vibe, depending on what posture you put forth. Slouching, for instance, is a classic sign of lack of confidence.

## Rubbing Any Body Part

People often do this when they are not comfortable. They could rub their fingers, neck, face, hair, or leg. It is a classic sign of discomfort when a person is not comfortable with the topic of conversation or is super nervous. It could also be someone hiding information, hence trying to keep themselves calm by such self-soothing behavior.

## Barriers

When we are uncomfortable with the person we are talking to or the subject of conversation, there is a chance that we create a barrier between us. This barrier could be body parts, like the arms, legs, or objects. Someone who holds a briefcase tightly against their chest when communicating is clearly showing a blocking behavior.

## Fidgeting

This is a classic sign of negative energy. Fidgeting is the body involuntarily trying to escape an uncomfortable situation. Examples are tapping of the feet and drumming of the hands. People could do this consciously or unconsciously when bored. It is also a sign of impatience with the person or conversation.

# Chapter 5: How to Show Yourself to Others

After you can discover all of the methods that people are communicating with you through their bodies, you can learn how to use your body to convey particular messages. We have our mouths and our minds to share valuable information, but we can be very influential and powerful through our bodies as well. We will talk about all the ways that you can persuade and influence people based on using your different body language methods.

## Making Good Impressions

Now that you are a master at reading body language, it's time to learn how you can use it for your benefit. When you're able to take your body language and find a way that you can use to get the things that you want, you will be an expert in persuasion. You can help friends out by improving their mood, you can talk to your boss and be confident enough to get the things that you want, and you can generally be a more likable person who attracts different people in your life.

One of the first things that you'll want to do with your body language is to learn how to make proper connections. You want to have the right first impression so that people get a good sense of who you are from the very beginning. The people who might think that everybody hates them in the world and has trouble making friends might simply be somebody who has impoverished body language. They could be a person that's closed off and has no interest in talking to other people, to the point that they don't even make eye contact or smile when meeting new individuals.

The first thing that you'll want to do is make sure that you show confidence, you don't necessarily need to be some amazingly talented person who everybody becomes envious of; you simply want to have a certain level of trust, so that people understand when they look at you, that you believe in yourself. Why should anyone want to get to know you when you aren't even comfortable with who you are on an individual level? You can show this confidence through your body language by having a puffed-up chest, your shoulders back in, and standing or sitting up straight. You can also make sure that you have a firm handshake from the moment that you make contact with them. Use the right amount of eye contact to let them know that you're listening to them.

You don't want to have your hands in your pockets or hide your hands in a professional setting. In a more casual environment, it's not that big of a deal. We were probably often told by our parents to keep our hands out of our pockets because it makes us look untrustworthy. While that can be true, if you're meeting new friends it's not as big of a deal. Make sure that you act welcoming, keep your body open, and have a warm, friendly smile. Put your hand or arms out if they want to come in for a hug. Some people like making that first initial connection.

Stand in front of this other person and keep your body across from each other. You want to make sure that the person that you're communicating with is on the same level as you. You don't want to stand over somebody who's sitting down, and you don't want to stay sitting while somebody is standing looking down at you.

Mirror their body language so that they can feel connected to you. If you're acting in the same way that they are, then they're going to be more recognizable of your different actions.

In general, make sure that you're doing your best to make them feel comfortable. It's your personality that's going to attract somebody. It's the way that you can make them laugh or the exciting things that you have to share with them. That will keep them coming back. At the same time if you're closed off and not offering any positive or healthy body language from the beginning, then they might not be as willing to get to know who you are.

## Sending Signals to Others

Aside from making good impressions, we also might want to send certain signals to other people.

There are a few different ways that you can send better messages by using your body alone. The first thing that you'll want to do is make sure first that you pick up on who you're trying to convince. Is it an entire audience or a large group of people, or are you simply trying to be more persuasive on a one-to-one level? Whatever the situation might identify those people around you who you might be trying to persuade. After this, start to pick up on how other people are interacting. Be aware of their little body language movements. Do they have microexpressions that are showing their emotions? Are they sitting in a certain way? Notice these little things and get a quick speed read of the way that they're all using their bodies. Then notice the ways that you're using your own body. Are you showing anger, frustration, annoyance, happiness, sadness, etc. in the way that you're interacting with them? Once you get a quick reading of both your and their body language, it's time to start to mirror everybody.

Mirror them so that they feel more connected to you. They're going to snap into focus with you and your body when they recognize that you're using it in the same way that they're using theirs. Once you've done this, now it is your chance to change your body language so that you can change others. What types of signals are you trying to send? Do you want them to feel more comfortable and romantically connected to you? This is when you can break the barrier and get a little bit flirtier in the same breath. Are you trying to persuade them and put them in a better mood so that they are more agreeable to something that you might be talking about? This is when you could use a little touch of their shoulder, maybe a laugh or smile, or a comprehensive posture to show that you're open and willing to talk and communicate with them. Whatever it might be that you're trying to do, look at your intention and figure out how you can persuade them using your body language. This is going to be the best way that you can send positive signals to other people.

## Showing Confidence

You don't have to be a confident person to show confidence. Sometimes only showing that faith and building yourself up in that way can be enough to get you to a place where you do feel confident. It's like how you might look in the mirror and smile and help yourself get into a better mood. This is simple enough to make it easier for you to change your emotion based on one small action.

The same can be said for building confidence. If you look confident, that might eventually come afterward. Even if you still feel anxious at the end of the day, then this at least helps others overlook that anxiety and instead see the compassion in your eyes.

The first thing you'll want to do is make sure that you stand up straight. Keep your chin up and your eyes wide. Try not to look down at people, to the point where your chin is pointing towards the sky. Simply ensure that it's not touching your neck and that you're not keeping your head down. You are in control of your body and the situation. Keep your shoulders back so that your chest is out a little bit more. You don't need to look like a soldier standing there stiffly, but the more you slouch, the less confidence that you'll have. Make sure that you show your hands and keep your arms open. You don't want to be closed off and make it seem as though you're not approachable. Though you might think it's better to be a little bit closed off to be confident, it's best to have an open demeanor. Just because you're free and willing to communicate through your body doesn't mean that you're passive or going to be easily persuaded through your verbal language. It's just a way to set you up so that it is easier to help convince other people by using your confident posture. Keep eye contact, but make sure that you are also looking around the room and getting a good sense of how everybody is feeling. The more confidence you show, the more that you'll feel it, and this can improve your life drastically.

# Chapter 6: How to Identify Insecurity

When you spot someone behaving irrationally, it's easy to dismiss them as being emotional or dramatic. Very rarely do we stop to consider that perhaps this might be a sign of insecurity. Instead of analyzing their body language to get the full picture and trying to empathize with them, we either choose to ignore them, dismiss them, or even get annoyed if their irrational behavior is affecting us directly. We don't pause long enough to consider that this behavior could be their way of trying to cover up their emotional insecurity.

Your ability to spot insecurity can be advantageous to you in several situations. Negotiation, conflict resolution, and even within a problem-solving dynamic. There are several reasons why insecurity could manifest. People can be insecure about their looks, money, power, and most of the time, these insecurities can be difficult to manage when you don't know how to identify them. Once you do though, it gives you leverage that you can use to connect with the person on a level to which they can relate. In a negotiation situation, this can be extremely useful in swinging the odds in your favor. Being able to spot insecurity is also going to serve you well in terms of protecting yourself. Sometimes, these insecure individuals have strong, negative energy about them, and it is easy to get swept up in their emotional turmoil and become insecure yourself if you spend enough time around them. A lack of eye contact, the nervous pacing, hunched posture, biting of the fingernails in some cases, repeatedly touching certain parts of the body like the neck, and fidgeting are obvious signs of insecurity and discomfort. Aside from the obvious body language that they display, keep your eyes peeled for the following signs that signal you're dealing with an insecure individual:

- **They make you feel insecure too:** Their insecurity will be so strong it starts to rub off on you. You'll want to exercise caution here, since beginning to doubt yourself is going to make you easy prey to manipulators.
- **Constant worry:** They're constantly worried that every decision they make is going to reflect badly on them. They express concern about not knowing what the right thing to do is. They ask you want you to think several times, or even what you think they should do. They might apologize for being indecisive and unable to decide just yet.
- **Showing off:** Insecurity could also manifest itself in a different manner, where the insecure individual feels a constant need to show off their accomplishments just to make themselves feel better. Constantly brag about their amazing lifestyle, their wonderful shoes, their huge cars, and their elite education. All of this is done to

convince themselves that they have it all in a poor attempt to feel better about themselves.

- **Becoming defensive:** Insecure people become even more nervous, jittery, and on edge when they feel like they are being ganged up on or pressured into deciding. They'll be worried about offending you or making you angry with some of the choices they make, but they may become defensive if they feel like they're being attacked.
- **Frequent complaints:** There's always something to complain about when the whole world doesn't seem right to the insecure individual. They'll spend hours, days, weeks, or even months mulling over the concerns and worries, and find it hard to escape that "negative funk" they're in, no matter how much you try to coax them out of it. Even when there's nothing to complain about, they'll be the ones to find something wrong.
- **Indecisive nature:** They find it nearly impossible to make a decision and stick to it. They'll second guess, question, bounce from one choice to the next, and keep asking the same question repeatedly, almost as if they're having a hard time accepting the answers they're being given. Even if you gave them a possible solution, they'll reject your initial suggestion, but then come back and circle it again.

Mastering your emotions is essential to dealing with an insecure individual to avoid being easily influenced by their volatile, unpredictable emotional state. Compassion and empathy are especially important; what the insecure person needs is someone who can understand what they're going through. Not someone who is there to judge, criticize, or ridicule. Compassion requires a balanced approach so that our negative emotions are neither exaggerated nor suppressed when dealing with an insecure individual. This balancing act comes out from the process of relating our personal experiences with that of the suffering of others. Your ability to analyze their body language and read the unspoken communication that goes on is going to be your best asset in a time like this.

Insecurity is an emotional state that arises following a situation that is perceived as alarming or threatening. If the person confronted with this stimulus feels that their resources or skills are insufficient to manage and/or overcome the situation, they are likely to feel insecure. This emotion may manifest itself in the form of higher levels of anxiety, psychomotor agitation, allowing the person to feel unnerved but still able to mobilize extra resources to enable them to succeed. In these cases, insecurity has a protective effect in that it prevents us from making mistakes or taking unnecessary risks. For example, when one of the couples feels that their relationship is not safe, they can implement some strategies that, in their eyes, imply the solidification of the relationship, such as the promotion of dialogue, romantic outings, or even psychotherapeutic follow-up. Similarly, when a worker perceives their place as being at risk of being laid off, they will seek alternatives to avoid unemployment. But both in one context and the other insecurity can assume a higher level of intensity, no longer having such a protective effect.

In these cases, though is likely to be dominated by irrational beliefs, which grow spirally and produce a blocking effect. The person starts to live by what makes them insecure without, however, being able to find adjusted solutions. In the first example, this state of anxiety could translate into a set of behaviors that have both despair and nonsense, such as starting to search the partner's cell for signs of a potential extramarital relationship, aggressive and/or controlling comments, etc. In the following example, it could happen that the person would be so depressed that they would not invest either in the current job or in the search for a new placement, allowing insecurity to have the blocking effect.

# Chapter 7: Benefits of Personality Analysis

## When to Analyze People

Analyzing people is one of those skills that can be used in almost any context. You can use it at work, in personal relationships, politics, religion, and even just in day-to-day life. Because of this versatility, you may find that you are constantly analyzing people, which is okay. Remember, your unconscious mind already makes snapshot judgments about other people and their intentions, so you were already analyzing people, to begin with. Now, you are simply making an effort to ensure that those analyses are made in your conscious mind so you can be aware of them.

Now, let's take a look at several different compelling situations in which being able to analyze someone is a critical skill to know consciously:

- **In parenting:** When you can analyze other people, you can begin to use those skills toward your children. Now, you may be thinking that a child's mind is not sophisticated enough to get a reliable read on, but remember, the child's feelings are usually entirely genuine. In essence, they have the feeling that they have, and though the reason behind those feelings may be less than compelling to you as a parent, that does not in any way dismiss the feelings. By recognizing the child's emotions, you can begin to understand what is going on in your child's mind, and that will allow you to parent calmly and more effectively.
- **In relationships:** When you live with someone else, it can be incredibly easy to step on someone else's toes without realizing it. Of course, constantly stepping on the toes of someone else is likely to lead to some degree of resentment if it is never addressed. Yet, some people have a hard time talking when they are uncomfortable or miserable. This is where being able to analyze someone else comes in—you will tell what your partner's base emotions are when you interact, allowing you to play the role of support.
- **In the workplace:** Especially if you interact with other people, you need to analyze other people. You will see how your coworkers view you, allowing you to change your behaviors to get the company image that you desire. Beyond just that, you may also work in a field that requires you to get good reads on someone in the first place.

- **In public:** When you interact with people in public, you need to be able to protect yourself. When you can read other people, you can determine whether you are safe or whether someone is threatening or suspicious. This means that you can prepare yourself no matter the situation to ensure that you are always ready to respond.

## Why Analyze People

There is no formula to analyze people around or with you. Some people understand based on their gestures, body language, verbal communication, non-verbal communication, and how they walk and dress up. To begin with, you can consider the following:

- Studying yourself.
- Understanding the nature of the person you are trying to analyze.
- Scrutinizing their behavior.
- Focusing on the words of another person.
- Knowing body language.
- Getting acquainted with cultural differences.
- Concentrating on social skills.
- Forming a general assumption on the nature of a person.
- Interpretation of verbal communication and pattern.
- Knowing the reason behind their type of personality.
- Having an elementary overview of the personality of an individual.

Why is it important to understand a personality? If you are ambitious, then yes, it is important to read the other person, but if you do not want any growth professionally and you are happy with a 9–5 p.m. job, it is not your cup of tea. Likewise, if you value your relationships, analyzing folks is important. Analyzing people is of immense importance from the perspective of life more than any other realm like professionally.

The more finely you understand yourself and other folks around, the more booming you will be in dealing with the circumstances and people and getting things on the right track. Understanding personalities is an unexpectedly comprehensive and practical subject than psychology. It is an extensive word comprising of psychology and implementing the analysis to day to day advantage in everyday circumstances. It is vital to stay with family and amongst friends as well as colleagues. Learn it to be the best and different of all members of a group. Get it to attract people, to help, to support, to influence, to raise your voice and to express your point of view, to understand better, to make a right and fast decision, to encourage people, to manage people, to direct folks, to solve the conflicts and most importantly to portray the right personality of ourselves.

## Advantages of Analyzing People

People are an open book that needs little attention to understand their traits. By closely observing what they do, what they say, and listening to what others are saying reveals a pretty good picture of their attitude and personality. It has proven to be effective and true in most cases. Attend them is the best you can do as a friend, family member, colleague, or boss in the office. Analysis of people, behavior, body language and gesture are fascinating because of diverse learning experiences based on traits or behavior adopted by a person. Therefore, it is significant and essential to be successful in different walks of life like a business arena, day-to-day life, companionships, relationships, etc.

Let us have a quick look at the advantage that results due to the analysis of people:

- Analysis of people offers an individual the knowledge of skills required to deal with people. It mostly throws light on tips to conduct with positivity.
- It assists in recognizing, realize and uphold human life and its standpoint, thereby shun conflicts.
- It helps an individual develop understanding and sympathy towards others and results in a reduction of people from getting judgmental and restricts them from pointing the finger at others.
- It fabricates a healthy society enabling people to evaluate themselves before judging others.

Every individual to succeed in life requires important interpersonal and communication skills to stand at a pioneering position in the corporate sector and in a society that is always changing. In today's time when students and people migrate out for jobs and studies, the study of the analysis of people is quite handy to understand people abroad and minimize the possibility of deception.

Study of people is a type of preparation tool to cope with the colleagues at the office and work efficiently at work front and social life.

It aids in comprehending the presence of imperfection in their life which can be improved by understanding the behavior of the other person and following their good features.

We live in a society where people of different personalities, beliefs, attitudes, perceptions, and behaviors are found. Their analysis helps to get aware of the techniques to deal with them. It can be immensely helpful for people at the management level in picking up the right employees by understanding their employees' behavior. Through analysis, you can project, direct, alter and control the distinct behavior of an individual. Through analysis of people, you can get an idea of their reaction to a particular situation in advance and prepare for the situation. Analysis of people is helpful for the successful conduct of society and accomplishment of goals.

It is conceivable they have a legitimate concern, yet you will possibly observe that you can be quiet and target. So don't discard the good along with the bad. In any case, ensure you are quiet and objective and are taking a gander at all the conceivable outcomes you think about before making any move.

You may jump at the chance to get a subsequent sentiment or do some examination yourself. You might originate from an extraordinary attitude. Maybe a more beneficial one.

One thing is sure; however, when you are made to feel remorseful or stressed on account of your activities, you are not being treated with deference. Perhaps it's an ideal opportunity to discover somebody who will.

## How to Analyze Others With Mind Control

The capability to analyze a person is one of the most valuable skills one can possess. People that you interact with every day send you signals, and if you learn and pay attention to the signals that they send you without them knowing, you will be able to analyze and read people easily. Each person experiences similar basic human needs—relationships, recognition, regimentation, and outcome—with others having more dominance than others.

Most signals—visuals, vocal and verbal will be available to you when you slow down or speed up, when you concentrate on the details or when you work on building relationships.

Here are some techniques that you can use to analyze someone's personality in an instant:

- Pay close attention to the person's handwriting and text messages. When you compare the amount of negative and positive words, then you can illustrate large changes in an individual's personality. People who use more swear words than common words tend to be more agreeable; extroverts tend to use words with positive connotations. Conscientious bloggers will tend to use words about achievement.

- Pay attention to their smile. It is understood that people with a sincere smile are more likely to be married, be happier, stays married, and enjoy better health throughout their lives compared to those with smiles perceived to be fake smiles.
- Look at their sleep schedule. People with a morning-type schedule will tend to be more focused and introverted. While, people with an evening type of schedule will tend to be more prepared to take risks, less likely to confirm, and have a far more creative, impulsive outlook of life.
- Note the type of music they listen to. You will realize that musical choices can predict personalities across four main categories:
    - Rhythmic and energetic music, for example, hip-hop, rap, and electronica are agreeable, liberal, politically, and they are not afraid to speak their mind, and mostly they are extroverted.
    - Those that love conventional and upbeat kinds of music, for example, pop music, country, and religious, are agreeable, but they are not open. Extroverts are often rich, athletic, and politically conservative.
    - Complex and reflective kinds of music, for example, blues, jazz, and classical, indicate that a person is more open, above-average intelligence, and more emotionally stable.
    - Rebellious and intense kinds of music, for example, rock, heavy metal, and alternative suggest that the person is more open, above-average intelligence, and athletic.
- Left-handed. A left-handed person could be predicted by low levels of testosterone exposure, which is related to a high level of empathy. Left-handed men are often creative, generous, and empathetic. They also excellently perform when it comes to activities that need a rapid transfer of information, leadership experience, and they tend to have higher wages.
- Conservatives in their bedrooms may suggest their politics. Conservatives' rooms tend to be more organized and structured; their rooms contain conventional decorations, for example, flags, alcohol bottles, and sports paraphernalia. On the contrary, liberal rooms contained a large number of varieties of books, art supplies, movie tickets, travel and cultural memorabilia, and music CDs.

# Chapter 8: How Body Language Enhances Your Mind

Our body language is the way we speak with our outside world—and the more significant part of us doesn't understand, we are doing it! Body language phenomenally affects the center of who you are as an individual. It impacts our posture and physiological wellbeing, yet it can likewise change our psychological viewpoint, the impression of the world, and others' perception of us.

## How Our Body Imparts

We utilize our body language to communicate our musings, thoughts, and feelings; we synchronize body developments to the words we express. We impart purposefully through activities like shrugging our shoulders or applauding just as through inadvertent correspondence like twisting in on ourselves or guiding our feet an alternate way toward the individual we are talking to.

## Force Presenting

One of the significant specialists in the zone of body language is Amy Cuddy. In her TedTalk, Cuddy talks about how body language can contrast among succeeding and coming up short at prospective employee meet-ups. She made members remain in high force stances and low force models for two minutes before sending them into a top weight talk with the condition. She estimated levels of the pressure hormone cortisol and the predominance hormone testosterone. The outcomes demonstrated that those remaining in high force present had expanded testosterone degrees and lower cortisol levels than those in little force present.

## Improve Your Posture to Improve Your Temperament

Body language likely isn't the first sport you'd think to look at when experiencing a low state of mind. However, investigating our body language can reveal to us how we are truly feeling. Our body language has an immediate connection to our temperament, similarly that our mindset influences our posture.
Simple ways you can fix your posture to adjust your state of mind:

- Smile when you are having a terrible day!
- Unfold your arms when you feel anxious and permit yourself to be available to circumstances.
- Turning the palms of your hands forward when you walk will urge the shoulders to unwind back as opposed to moving advances.
- Power present before pressure instigating situations like prospective employee meet-ups.

## Getting and Understanding Non-Verbal Signals

Lauren murmured. She'd quite recently gotten an email from her chief, Gus, saying that the item proposition she'd been taking a shot at would not have been closed down all things considered. It didn't bode well. Seven days prior, she'd been in a gathering with Gus, and he'd appeared to be extremely positive about everything. Of course, he hadn't looked, and he continued watching out of the window at something. In any case, she'd recently put that down to him being occupied. Furthermore, he'd said that "the task will most likely stretch the go-beyond."

On the off chance that Lauren had discovered somewhat progressively about body language, she'd have understood that Gus was attempting to reveal to her that he wasn't "sold" on her thought. He simply wasn't utilizing words.

## Troublesome Conversations and Defensiveness

Troublesome or tense deliberations are an awkward unavoidable truth grinding away. Maybe you've needed to manage an annoying client, or expected to converse with somebody about their terrible showing. Or then again perhaps you've arranged a significant agreement.

In a perfect world, these circumstances would be settled tranquility. Be that as it may, regularly, they are entangled by sentiments of apprehension, stress, preventiveness, or even resentment. Also, however, we may attempt to shroud them; these feelings regularly appear in our body language. For instance, on the chance that somebody is showing at least one of the accompanying practices, they will probably be withdrawn, uninvolved, or miserable:

- Arms collapsed before the body.
- Insignificant or tense outward appearance.
- The body got some distance from you.

- Eyes depressed, keeping in touch.
- Keeping away from unengaged audiences.

At the point when you have to convey an introduction or to work together in a gathering, you need the individuals around you to be 100% locked in. Here are some "obvious" signs that individuals might be exhausted or unbiased in what you're stating:

- Sitting drooped, with heads sad.
- Looking at something different, or into space.
- Squirming, picking at garments, or tinkering with pens and telephones.
- Composing or doodling.

## Establishing a Confident First Connection

These tips can assist you in adjusting your body language, so you establish an extraordinary first connection:

- **Have an open posture.** Be loose; however, don't slump! Sit or stand upstanding and place your hands by your sides. Abstain from remaining with your hands on your hips, as this will cause you to seem more significant, which can convey animosity or craving to rule.
- **Utilize a firm handshake.** However, don't become overly energetic! You don't need it to get unbalanced or, more regrettable, excruciating for the other individual. On the chance that it does, you'll likely seem to be impolite or forceful.
- **Keep in touch.** Try to maintain eye contact with the other person for a couple of moments one after another. This will give her that you're right and locked in. Be that as it may, abstain from transforming it into a gazing match!
- **Abstain from contacting your face.** There's a typical discernment that individuals who contact their appearances while addressing questions are being untrustworthy. While this isn't in every case valid, it's ideal to abstain from tinkering with your hair or contacting your mouth or nose, especially if your point is to seem to be reliable.

## Public Speaking

Positive body language can likewise assist you with engaging individuals, veil introduction nerves, and extending certainty when you talk in public. Here are many tips that can help you in doing this:

- **Have a positive posture.** Sit or stand upstanding, with your shoulders back and your arms unfurled and at your sides or before you. Try not to be enticed to place your hands in your pockets, or to slump, as this will make you look unbiased.
- **Keep your head up.** Your head ought to be upstanding and level. Inclining excessively far advance or in reverse can make you look forceful or self-important.

# Conclusion

Thank you for making it through to the end.

The next step is to get to the action and apply what you have learned from the book. Note that, learning how to analyze people is a wide topic that does not stop here. Therefore, it is beneficial for you to continue learning and find other equally beneficial resources where you can get the information you seek regarding how to analyze people. You understand that analyzing people does not have to be for unethical reasons, it is also possible to analyze people and use the information you gather ethically. For instance, you can analyze a client during a negotiation to know whether they are serious clients or not and also, to understand their references in the sales negotiation.

The bottom line is that we should not analyze people for unethical reasons. We should focus on using the information we gather from analyzing people to better react to their message and actions. It makes you seem smart and more in sync with people when you can react to their actions without overreacting simply because you understand what they wish to convey whether their words convey it effectively or not.

This book was designed to help you learn how to analyze people for a better environment and better relations with people. For instance, by understanding the different personality types, you are better able to comprehend and work with people who have different personalities without making anyone feel unwanted or not understood in every situation. As such, managers and leaders need to learn how to analyze people for the simple reason that they manage people with different personalities and they must ensure that everyone remains motivated to work and be productive.

Therefore, after gathering the much and beneficial information from this book, it is important for you to also teach the people around you how to analyze the people they work with and relate with daily. This is ethical in that; it helps people react to issues better as well as relationships with the people around them better. We all want to live in an accommodative world and we should be willing to do what it takes to achieve that. This includes helping people around us analyze other people's actions and reacting to them accordingly without hurting their feelings.

If at this point you are still wondering why you should invest extra time to understand how to analyze people, you could be avoiding the importance of identifying gestures, postures, and expressions that help you to be a better person as well. Moreover, if you wish to communicate your feelings without talking much or speaking, understanding the different body languages is the way to go. This is what most people apply when they refuse to talk to their partners and apply what they call "cold war." They let their actions and body language do the speaking and communicate what they feel. In the end, the partner understands that they are not happy about something and they either ask how to change things or better still do what is required of them. This is the perfect example of how a person can apply body language and how people can read body language in a bid to save a situation.

www.ingramcontent.com/pod-product-compliance
Lightning Source LLC
Chambersburg PA
CBHW081625100526
44590CB00021B/3611